The History
and
Future of Faith

THE HISTORY
AND
FUTURE OF FAITH

Religion Past, Present, and to Come

ROBERT ELLWOOD

CROSSROAD · NEW YORK

1988

The Crossroad Publishing Company
370 Lexington Avenue, New York, N.Y. 10017

Copyright © 1988 by Robert Ellwood

Printed in the United States of America

Library of Congress Cataloging-in-Publication Data

Ellwood, Robert S., 1933–
The history and future of faith.

Includes index.
1. Religion.   2. Religions.   I. Title.
BL48.E428   1988   291   88-3860
ISBN 0-8245-0879-3

Contents

Preface

This is a book about the future of religion, looked at from the perspective of a historian of religion. In the way of historians, I have felt compelled to begin the topic at the beginning of human religion far in the remote past, and to carry its story from there up to the present and beyond. This is therefore also a book about the origin and meaning of human religion.

The History and Future of Faith was many years in the making, and as I have tried to think through the tangled web of issues it has raised, it has gone through several changes of concept. Chapters 5 and 6 were originally presented as a paper at a conference on "Religion and Modernity," at the University of British Columbia in December 1981. This paper has recently appeared under the title "Modern Religion as Folk Religion," in *Modernity and Religion,* edited by William Nicholls.[1]

The writing was essentially completed in South Africa in the fall of 1986, while I was serving as visiting professor in the Department of Religious Studies at the University of Cape Town. I am deeply grateful to this faculty for the honor of their invitation, for affording me quiet time for writing, and above all for numerous helpful suggestions and critiques as I presented much of this material in graduate and faculty seminars. I am also grateful to the faculty of the Department of Religious Studies at the University of Natal, Pietermaritzburg, South Africa, for a most useful discussion of the same material during a briefer visit to that campus.

1. SR Supplements 19, Canadian Corporation for Studies in Religion (Waterloo, Ont.: Wilfred Laurier University Press), pp. 19–44.

In thanks and tribute to these two fine departments of religious studies, I would like to inscribe words cited by the late distinguished South African Christian and novelist Alan Paton in an unfinished essay penned only a few days before his death. They are from a tablet in an old English church: ". . .When throughout England all things sacred were either profaned or neglected, this church was built by Sir Robert Shirley, Bart., whose special praise it is to have done the best things in the worst times and to have done the best things in the worst times and to have hoped them in the most calamitous."[2]

2. Alan Paton, "A Literary Remembrance," *Time* 131, 17 (April 25, 1988).

Chapter 1

Religion Today and Tomorrow

What future, if any, has religion on planet earth?

Whatever the answer, we can be sure that it is in no small part being shaped today. The religious life of Buck Rogers's twenty-fifth century is being prepared by the thoughts, words, and deeds of countless personages great and small on earth now, even as the long shadows of Renaissance humanists and Protestant reformers of more than four centuries ago still fall over much of the spiritual world today.

But as to what really is happening in religion now, reports vary considerably. This is partly because evidence concerning a matter ultimately so deeply rooted in the secret places of subjectivity, however much it may be outwardly expressed, is extremely hard to assess. It is also because religion, the redoubt of myth and belief, generates myths and nonempirical beliefs about its own past and present as avidly as it does about the supernatural. In the eyes of critics and believers alike, a religion may be world conquering or a voice from the past, when the truth is more likely to be a muddle in the middle than at some such dramatic extreme.

Thus there are those, both religionists and others, who contend that faith is obviously in decline. Ours, they insist, is much less than a mustard seed of belief compared with the fervor of our forefathers and foremothers. But the piety of the past has been a stock-in-trade of religion from the Hebrew prophets, and the ancient Buddhist notion of the decline of the Dharma or the Hindu of the Kali-yuga, to the nineteenth-century idealization of medieval faith among Catholic romantics or the unquestioning

1

American belief in the belief of the Founding Fathers. No doubt more than half of the pious past is a religious myth produced because present religion needs it, perhaps as an extension of the myth of a golden age or an unfallen primal state. The evils of the present to which religion feels called to point are all the better showcased against a more godly past, and the divine origins of the faith are better legitimated if its first fruits are portrayed as unambiguously virtuous. Yet the actual data for the extent of past devotion and practice, scanty as it is, raises hard questions.

In odd alliance with the religious myth of the pious past is the secular, social science idea of secularization. Essentially the notion that religion is being replaced by worldly, especially scientific, views of reality and clues to appropriate human action, secularization as an idea no doubt reflects some sort of truth. At the same time, as an account of reality that expresses in historical narrative form the paradigm by which its devotees themselves work and live, it can in a technical sense be called a myth. For in religious studies, the term *myth* does not imply a judgment on whether a narrative is true or not, but on its function within its culture; a myth is not a casual fable or entertainment, but an embodiment in story form of certain basic values and ultimate reality perceptions. In the words of the postmodernist critics to whom we shall later turn, the story of the decline of religion and rise of science is a Grand Narrative, an epic whose overall sweep—in the eyes of its tellers—overshadows any contrary particulars.

On the other hand are those for whom religion is advancing, or at least holding its own about as well as ever. These are, first, the triumphalists of all faiths who, like the sundial, count only the sunny hours. Their notice registers only the up statistics, and they joyfully see the world turning their way; it is bound to fall before the next evangelistic crusade or with the maturation of the Aquarian generation.

In addition to the triumphalist, two other sanguine readings of the religious future are available, which may be termed empirical and philosophical. On the empirical front, one can point to spotty but significant evidence that the religiosity of the past was not on such a high level as the mythologies make it appear. Religion's present strength, in fact, may represent less a decline than just a perpetuation of what—shorn of glamor—the case has always been, and so presage religion as respectable a future as it has ever had.

All historians know, for example, that the American republic was not founded wholly by devout Christians but by a motley array of believers, skeptics, deists, and sheer worldlings. Most of the Founding Fathers were deeply affected, to say the least, by the Enlightenment's deism. Society as a whole, after the Great Awakening but prior to the popular evangelical revivals of the nineteenth century, was represented by far less than half its numbers on church membership rolls at the time of the American Revolution. Among vast segments of the population—southern slaves, on the frontier, in urban slums—spiritual life was tenuous and chaotic even if capable of being stirred up. Thomas Jefferson enjoined only the ethical teachings of Jesus, preparing his own abridged New Testament to this end, and expected that by the end of his life Unitarianism would be universally adopted because of its superior rationality. Benjamin Franklin, in 1790, the year he died, affirmed belief in one God, Creator of the universe, but added: "As to Jesus . . . I have . . . some doubts as to his divinity; though it is a question I do not dogmatize upon, having never studied it, and think it needless to busy myself with it now, when I expect soon an opportunity to knowing the truth with less trouble."[1] Needless to add, public opinions of this order would be political suicide for any American statesman of the 1980s and leave us wondering which way secularization, or the disentanglement of religion from the state that Jefferson and Franklin so devoutly desired, has gone.

Or suppose we go back to the Middle Ages, the "Age of Faith." Meticulous work in social history is now beginning to paint a picture of popular religion up to the eve of the Reformation rather different from the conventional vision of a sea of Catholic piety. We perceive a population only lightly Christianized, in which various disorganized but potent pagan carry-overs were at least as trusted as the Church, and in which even in the best of times sizable components of people—in mountainous or wooded backcountry, among an underclass of rural and urban poor— were hardly touched by the faith at all, save on the most casual and quasi-magical level. Very often, of course, it was not the best of times in medieval Europe, and infidel invasion, feudal war, famine, and plague would completely disrupt ecclesiastical life. At the same time, the appeal of spiritual enthusiasms, largely heretical, was never to be discounted among the hard-pressed masses.

Emmanuel Le Roy Ladurie, in his valuable study of late medieval life in the southern French community of Montaillou and its environs, indicates that although baptism was virtually universal and church festivals were popular, only about half the population attended church on an average Sunday—a figure comparable to the 40 percent pollsters get for the United States in the 1980s. Le Roy Ladurie comments: "There is nothing surprising about this lukewarm attitude. Specifically Christian piety was always the attribute of an elite in the Middle Ages and even when, in time of panic, this elite grew very numerous, it still remained urban rather than rural, and did not include the mountain dwellers."[2]

Even among the elite, one might add, chivalry was no less a potent force than the faith, and one whose values were not seldom at odds with it. William Marshall, first earl of Pembroke and a powerful political figure under several English kings, was urged by a cleric upon his deathbed in 1219 to sell some eight fine robes and give the money to the poor for the salvation of his soul; the earl declined, saying he was obliged to give them to the knights who had served him. He also refused to return his tournament winnings for the assurance of heaven, saying, "If because of this the kingdom of God is closed to me, there is nothing I can do about it." But he added that the teachings of the priests on such matters must be false, "else no one would be saved."[3] Such attitudes were by no means atypical of the medieval lay aristocracy, who (with some exceptions, such as the frankly nonreligious William "Rufus" II of England) may have professed Christ but whose real moral culture was that of the tournament ground and the blood-stained field of honor.

Returning to Montaillou, Le Roy Ladurie cites examples of actual unbelievers as well as the indifferent among the common people of the thirteenth and fourteenth centuries. There were those who denied God, the soul, and the afterlife. One peasant said that the soul consisted merely of blood and therefore disappeared after death, heaven being when you were happy in this world and hell when you were miserable, and that was all there was to it.[4]

To be sure, Montaillou was in a part of France heavily affected by the Albigensian or Cathar heresy; the detailed information the modern author is able to present is derived for the most part from testimony presented at a bishop's court inquiring into this problem. But it corroborates other opinions that lead us to doubt whether any picture of religion on a terminal downslide since a medieval high point can be wholly credited. Keith Thomas, in his magisterial *Religion and the Decline of Magic,* concludes: "We do not know enough about the religious beliefs and practices of our remote ancestors to be certain of the extent to which religious faith and practice have actually declined."[5]

Likewise, it would be false to think things were much different in premodern India, China, Japan, or in the Islamic world. Here too the lay upper classes generously mixed their Hindu, Buddhist, Confucian, or Muslim faith with knightly or other worldly values; and for the vast lower classes, when the sheer struggle for survival did not shoulder out all other concerns, religion like bread itself was a haphazard thing, usually only an aspect of, and subordinate to, identity as a member of family and village.

Some were devout, some were superstitious, but many then as now were religious only in the sense that, in their illiteracy, they were not self-consciously unbelievers in the only spiritual culture they knew, and could be counted on to swell the crowds at great religious processions and festivals. What supernatural beliefs and rites impinged on their lives were at least from out of the same cultural world as the official religion, though perhaps distorted, ill understood, or remnants of earlier eras.

Over against this picture, optimists for religion can perceive ways in which religion may well be more deeply rooted now than then. Bishops and mandarins may not exercise the political influence of bygone days, but on the other hand the spread of literacy means that far more believers have a clearer idea of what they believe; understanding a faith enhances commitment as often as it disillusions. Vastly improved transportation makes the practice of religion accessible in its fullness as never before. The mountain and forest people, excluded in the Middle Ages, can now drive to church in a pickup if they wish. Many times past numbers can now make the pilgrimage to Mecca, Rome, Jerusalem, or Banaras by charter jet. One need only mention the religious impact of the electronic media. The vast technological revolutions that have changed the Middle Ages, and the eighteenth century, into the modern world have had, in other words, a complex and ambivalent impact on religion. Undoubtedly the intellectual questions raised by the science behind this technology, and the massive disruption of traditional patterns of life it has entailed, have unsettled the faith of many. Yet science and technology have served on other fronts to buttress religion. As we shall see, the jury is still out on the question of whether the conditions of the modern world are really advantageous or detrimental for religion—not religion as it was in the Stone Age or the twelfth century, but religion as it might be able to adapt itself to the twentieth century and the twenty-first.

Turning to philosophical visions of the religious future, we will focus our attention on such modern sages as Hegel, Aurobindo, and Teilhard de Chardin, who have foreseen a future in which humans become more spiritual until, in an ultimate eschatological consummation, the promises of religion are fulfilled. These positions are not based so much on fideistic belief in the indefectibility of Church, Bible, or true praxis, as on a belief in the ultimate reality of the subject of religion, God, or spirit, and its necessary ultimate self-realization.

Georg W. F. Hegel saw all of human history as a process of the unfolding of *geist*, spirit, within humanity through stages of religious development and the evolution of human self-knowledge and freedom (which are the same thing). The ultimate end of the course of history is the merger of religion and the state—that is, the creation of a society in which religion need have no separate existence, since it and all beings in it are sacred, free, and self-knowing, their spiritual reality fully actualized. Religion gives way to philosophy, the most absolute because the most abstract, departicularized form of knowledge, for, as J. N. Findlay has put it in describing Hegel's position, "The ultimate fate of all imaginative religious presentations is therefore to hand over their majesty and authority to self-conscious Spirit, that the latter may be all in all. . . . The God outside of us who saves us by His grace, is a misleading pictorial expression for saving forces *intrinsic* to self-conscious Spirit, wherever this may be present."[6]

The Hindu sage Sri Aurobindo Ghose (1872–1950) proposed a comparable view of things. The evolution of the world, he taught, is the return of Brahman, God, to himself. God himself is impelling this process, but human beings through the practice of yoga can accelerate it in themselves and for the entire race by awakening more quickly the "supermind," which makes us fully God-realized individuals and completes the divine process; ultimately all beings will be so realized and a divine universe attained. Indeed, the sage said, we are now at a critical point in this process, for evolution cannot stand still, yet in the case of beings as intelligent as humans their cooperation is required. Humans must now elect to move on to realize the supermind within their grasp, or our kind will find itself cast aside and a more amenable species taking the vanguard role in divine self-realization. As A. B. Patel said in support of Aurobindo's concept, "If man in his egoism thinks that he is the last summit of evolution, he is sadly mistaken. Evolution still proceeds, and in the course of time a being will appear on this planet who will be advanced as present man is beyond ape. . . . A being with supramental or truth consciousness."[7]

Although contemporaries, Aurobindo and the French Jesuit Pierre Teilhard de Chardin (1881–1955) moved in different worlds and may never have heard of each other more than in passing. But their thought shows remarkable structural similarity and has often been compared. Like the Indian, Teilhard was profoundly concerned to reconcile the spirit of modern science, particularly its evolutionism, with a religious perspective that saved the spiritual nature of humanity and affirmed God as the ultimate source and end of all. Teilhard saw universal evolution as a "cosmogenesis" moving to greater and greater levels of complexity represented by the emergence of life, and of mind from an "inwardness" latent in matter, all culminating in a Point Omega when the "noosphere," or realm of thought/spirit, will reach its final ecstasy and liberation, transcendence of the material in God. That is an inconceivable goal, yet the magnet of all that has or will happen. "No one would dare to picture to himself what the noosphere will be like in its final guise, no one, that is, who has glimpsed however faintly the incredible potential of unexpectedness accumulated in the spirit of the earth."[8] But God will be all in all.

A contemporary American thinker who, from the perspective of psychological philosophy, has gone in the same direction is Ken Wilbur. Like the others, he has sensed that humankind is now at some point of critical juncture in the evolution of consciousness, and that the past and future of religion is intimately bound up with this crisis. Thus far, Wilbur tells us, human development has been in the direction of increased rationality and the emergence of an ego-centered human consciousness, projects that free mind from subservience to the body and the various subrational centers of the emotions and the brain. The advance toward reason and ego may seem to be a move away from religion, but that is only if religion is identified with the prerational or pre-ego styles of consciousness. For the present ego-centered human consciousness is itself only a stage toward something more: call it transrational, transegoic, or transpersonal. Wilbur is strongly critical of what he calls the "pre/trans fallacy," confusing that which went before the ego stage of consciousness with what will follow it, and will be aware of far more dimensions of reality than ego ever can be. The transego state, he tells us, is adumbrated by the mystical traditions within the several religions; its fuller emergence will be impelled by contradictions between subjective and outer experience that ego-consciousness can register but cannot resolve on its own terms.[9]

All these thinkers indicate a future for religion, or at least for the ground of religion in the human spirit, though they imply considerable change in religion's role. The suggestion is that, as people become more generally spiritual, the structures of religious sociology, rite, and belief as we now know them will wither away, being obsolete.

This outlook is by no means entirely modern. It can be traced back at least as far as the medieval Joachim of Flora, with his apocalyptic talk of a forthcoming "Age of the Spirit." Nor is the idea of formal religion being transcended only restricted to marginal thinkers of dubious orthodoxy. Although eschatology as historical evolution seems alien to all the great religions in their classic form, they do suggest that the real purpose of religion is, in fact, to self-destruct. For religion as a particular aspect of human psychology, human activity, and human society implies a dualism of sacred and profane. It is the dream of traditional religion as well as of Hegel, Aurobindo, Teilhard, and Wilbur to abolish that dualism so that all is undifferentiatedly sacred, and the glory of God covers the earth as the waters cover the sea.

According to the Book of Revelation, in the heavenly Jerusalem lowered to earth, no temple stands "for the Lord God Almighty and the Lamb are the temple of it." In the Hindu tradition, the *jivanmukta,* or God-realized man, has no need to worship in a temple or any other particular place, for God shines in him and he is in God always. In the words of the great sage Shankara, "The things perceived by the sense cause him neither grief nor pleasure. He is not attached to them. Neither does he shun them. Constantly delighting in the Atman he is always at play within himself. He tastes the sweet, unending bliss of the Atman and is satisfied."[10]

In the traditional religions, in contrast to the spiritual-evolution philosophies, the abolition of sacred and profane is attained either at an apocalyptic moment breaking into ordinary time and terminating it, or within "liberated" individuals in the midst of ordinary time, or rather as ordinary time continues as usual for others. In both the apocalyptic and personal-liberation frameworks, then, religion has no future different from its present short of world or personal eschaton; it is assumed that true religion, once revealed, will go on more or less as it is until the moment of absolute divine intervention for world or individual.

The modern philosophies of evolution of spirit, however, under the influence of historicism and biological evolutionary models, make the eschaton of religion's abolition so that God may be all in all a gradual process *within history,* and thus one that would bear directly on the future of religion. Indeed, most say the present historical moment is one of vital importance to the process. Presumably, if these thinkers are correct, we could expect to see the decline of religion on every hand, taking religion to mean separate, distinctive times and places of worship, social groups whether sects or churches, or even of discrete thoughts and experiences within the mind's continuum. While all this declines, we might expect to see people as a whole becoming more "spiritual"—more loving and more aware of God's presence everywhere, perhaps even gaining the remarkable yogic powers that Aurobindo postulates for those of supermind.

It is of course easy in this cynical age to ridicule such optimism and point to the still-sorry spiritual condition of the human species. But these philosophers, in their generous vision, are thinking of centuries and millennia, and beyond them the several billions of years left before the sun dies. We have arguably made some fitful moral and spiritual progress since the Old Stone Age; the

Crystal Cathedral, Garden Grove, California. Photograph courtesy of the Crystal Cathedral.

foresight of the spiritual evolutionists is not necessarily falsified if we do not see the Age of the Spirit dawn in tomorrow's headlines.

It is not our purpose at the moment, however, to assess the worth of these philosophies, or of the secularization theories to which we shall turn again shortly. (In passing, it is worth noting the odd convergence of spiritual evolution and secularization theory. Both postulate a fading away of religion as we now know it, replacing it with a more homogeneous human experience, whether of God or of the world.) First let us foreshorten our vision from far past and future to examine some data on the confusing state of religion in the late twentieth century.

To begin first with the Christian West, the primary fact that springs up before the eyes is the deep gulf between the postwar fate of religion in the United States and in the major industrialized nations of Western Europe with which one would think America would have most in common, at least on the surface. A 1975 Gallup Poll found that in the United States 56 percent of respondents claimed that religion was "very important" to them. (A 1986 poll found no significant change.) In Canada the comparable figure was 36 percent, and in Western Europe 27 percent. Furthermore, Europe has seen a sharp decline in religious practice since World War II, according to such polls and common observation, whereas in America the big story has been the persistence of religion at a high level, even though some areas of slight softening can be perceived. Thus in 1948 94 percent of Americans said they believed in God; in 1975 the figure was also 94 percent, and in 1984 was nine in ten. But in Scandinavia 81 percent made that profession in 1948, and in 1975 only 65 percent. In West Germany the percentage of God believers fell from 81 to 72 percent between 1968 and 1975.[11] Comparable figures for the other major industrialized nation, non-Christian Japan, consistently show an even lower level of religious importance and belief than for Western Europe, though polls in the late 1970s and early 1980s have suggested a bottoming out of decline and a slight but significant return to traditional Japanese values, including religious ones, as the island nation, perhaps surfeited with economic success, seems to be showing a new interest in finding its inner identity.

Comparison of poll figures on church attendance in the United States and Western Europe parallel the attitudinal data. These figures, going back to 1937, should be taken with some caution; polling techniques have improved considerably since the 1930s, and the question was not put in quite the same way at all times and in all places. Nonetheless the contrasts are dramatic enough to suggest overwhelmingly what is going on. In the United States the lowest year on record for church attendance was 1940, with 37 percent claiming attendance on an average Sunday. The high points were at 49 percent in the postwar religion boom years of 1955 and 1958. The turbulent sixties saw a steady decline to around 40 percent in 1971, and the index has stayed within a point or two of that ever since, into the 1980s.

In Great Britain it is another story. In 1937 the Gallup Poll found 78 percent of Britons church members, with 42 percent saying they attended church "regularly." But in 1947 only 30 percent said they had attended "last Sunday or the Sunday before last," and in 1957 just 14 percent claimed attendance "last Sunday."[12] Polls and observation concur in the view that British church attendance has stayed around that low figure since, or dropped even lower. Attendance in the other major Western European areas—France, Italy, Germany, Scandinavia—has similarly declined and is no higher than 15 percent in most communities on an average Sunday. There are, of course, pockets of resistance to the down-trend, such as Ireland. The situation in the Communist bloc, significantly, is far different, with church attendance levels in, say, Catholic Poland and Orthodox Rumania among the highest in the world.

The worldwide picture concerning religion gives equally mixed messages.[13] The Chinese revolution of 1949, which went far toward totally secularizing one-fourth of the world's population, radically revised world figures for the actual practice of religion. Traditional Chinese religion—a mix of Confucianism, Taoism, Buddhism, ancestrism, and folk religion—fell from a quarter of the world to 4.5 percent of the earth's population, projected to 2.5 percent in the year 2000. Because of losses in China and Indochina, Buddhism—as though to fulfill its own ancient prophecies about the decline of the Dharma—has declined from 7.8 percent of the world in 1900 to 6.3 percent in 1980. Hinduism, due to population increase in its Indian homeland, has held its own and increased slightly to 13.3 percent in 1980.

Despite losses in its traditional European home base, Christianity has spread in the twentieth century. In particular, it has reached in force more corners of the earth than any other religion, making it the most truly transcultural, universal religion in human history. It has flourished especially in sub-Saharan Africa and parts of Asia, there embracing new peoples as they made their way into modern nationhood and the ambiguities of the modern world. In the next century, it is said, Africa will be the demographic center of gravity for world Christendom.

Nonetheless, Christian triumphalism is given pause by several considerations. The European decline and any potential American decline leave one wondering if Christianity can long maintain itself in the pluralistic, computerized age into which we are moving; if it cannot, the vibrant faith of now-Christianized Third World societies may turn out to be only a phase in their movement from tribal animism to a "post-Christian" world, a transition all the more speedy for them because Christianity will be far less deeply rooted in their cultural heritage than it was in the cathedral squares and countrysides of Europe. We note also that the forms of Christianity growing fastest in the Third World are evangelical and pentecostal. However one assesses for oneself their spiritual value, it cannot be denied that historically these forms have tended to be religion "against culture" or "outside of culture," interacting poorly with a society's mainstream traditions of art, letters, and intellectual life. Compared with Orthodoxy, Catholicism, and classic or liberal Protestantism, they have inspired few great paintings, novels, or musical compositions, and engaged in little powerful dialogue with current philosophy. This is understandable, for they have usually found themselves religions of the oppressed or of the "common man" (even if he is sometimes economically successful) rather than of the intellectual or artistic elite. Whether, or in what way, they will ultimately become the spiritual foundations of affluent, successful, and culturally flourishing societies remains to be seen.

Despite its areas of growth, the portion of the world's population that is Christian declined from 34.4 percent in 1900 to 32.8 percent in 1980; this is the combined result of revolution, recedence in Western Europe, and higher birthrates in some other religious populations. But the youngest of the world-class religions, Islam, grew from 12.4 percent in 1900 to 16.5 percent in 1980, and is projected to reach nearly 20 percent in 2000. This is due to high birthrates, vigorous expansion, especially in Africa, and great tenacity among Muslim believers under Soviet and Chinese Communist rulers. Furthermore, it is well known that parts of the Islamic world have experienced unprecedented twentieth-century affluence, due mostly to oil money, and with it nearly everywhere an upsurge of confidence. There has been a reformation desire to build a true Islamic civilization. Sometimes the spirit has been militant and revolutionary; nearly always it has been accompanied by a mood of "reject the outside and return to the sources." Though beset with problems and contradictions like all religions in practice, any reflection on the future of religion cannot overlook the vitality and growth of Islam in the present.

Although the numbers are still small, since 1900 a significant growth has also obtained in the percentage of people adhering to "new religions"—from 0.4 percent at the turn of the century to 2.2 percent in 1980.

Finally, to complete the indicators-every-which-way picture, the most striking growth of all in the twentieth century has been in the number of persons who are atheist or totally nonreligious in practice—from an insignificant number in 1900 to 20.8 percent in 1980, projected to 21.3 percent in 2000. These figures, probably too conservative, represent partly the inroads of Western secularism, but even more, of course, the establishment of officially atheistic Communist regimes over one-third of the earth's population. How well they foreshadow the future depends on what sort of future these oft-troubled regimes have in anything like their current form, and how much they must make peace with faith their intellectual leadership despises. Even more important and portentious, we have in these populations the first large-scale test case in human history of whether wholly secular man can long endure, or whether overpowering subjective needs will sooner or later bring back religion in some guise.

The picture we have given of the religious situation should be sufficient to suggest its complexity. We shall now proceed to try to make some sense out of it. First we will survey the observation of religion, adding to it a discussion on how and when religion changes. That argument should be enough to suggest the big question, which will be the central concern of the rest of this book: have we in fact come to the end of a certain kind of religious history, however many loose ends may remain, so that in some sense at least the God of the future will be a God after the end of history?

But how, then, does one read the history of religion, and thereby talk about the future of religion, not to mention the future of God? In the last analysis, the issue is none other than the ancient problem of the one and the many. Is the universe best understood as a vast aggregation of parts, each moving by its own momentum, for which the whole is only an abstract generic concept? Or is it preeminently a unity, manifesting innumerable separate appearances as no more than epiphenomena?

Religion and science, on their respective levels, tend toward the latter, the primacy of the one: the unique divine mind, the unified field bound by mathematical constants. And if numbers unite, so do words. Despite the mighty capacity of human language to dualize and categorize experience so as to enjoin perception of the many as the "given," and oneness as no more than another trick of words, language also lays a groundwork for unity. Even before it divides up experience, it presupposes a common grammar to name the parts, and it comes out of a mind that knows itself, first, as a singular continuum of experience.

When it comes to history and human society, though, the one and the many seem more equally matched. In looking just at what human beings have done and are doing as parts of societies, we necessarily become aware that their experience continuums are manifold, as diverse as the human frames prowling our planet's surface. Yet at the same time each man or woman rarely functions in isolation. The experience each registers is largely experience involving other people. Further, it is mostly out of experience with others that one learns the calibrations by which to tune and assess even one's innermost subjectivity.

In this situation, then, as much can be said for the one as prior as for the many. The one can name the whole social unit, or alternatively the one single observer gazing out at it through the structuring apparatus of his or her mind—that apparatus itself conditioned, no matter how "scientific" the observer may profess to be, by the larger social "one" in all sorts of ways. The many, on the other hand, are the equal reality of society's innumerable diverse individuals.

In history, the one can be the whole sweep of historical experience, or again the one surveying eye. Or it may be the present instant, to which the whole previous panorama of instants are a manyness to be assimilated to the present, or seen as distant from it. Which is product of which? Is the individual the product of society or history, or is it the other way around?

Obviously the history or sociology of religion can be approached from either angle, as can the future of religion. One can see religion as a maze of diverse individual experiences, or talk of, say, "the history of the Church" or "the future of Hinduism." But the real point is that in religion, as in any real social entity, both possibilities contained in the foregoing unavoidable but unanswerable questions are true, and even to ask which side is prior is relatively meaningless. Religion is a social reality, and holds—indeed, epitomizes—the social/individual paradox. One can no more talk about religion without keeping both sides of the paradox in insoluble tension than, as we shall see, one can talk about the origin of religion apart from the origin of language and conceptual thought. Religion on the human scale emerged along with a combined process of human socialization and individuation, and short of some gradual or sudden eschaton it is unlikely to forget the habits of its nursery, though when it works well they may operate beneath the threshold of conscious mind.

A society or religion functioning with ideal lubricity would enact Peter Berger's externalization-objectification-internalization chain over and over so silently and smoothly people would be unaware of its movement.[14] Content within individual consciousness is projected outward to take shape in the public symbols of the city—the art and temples, the ruling beliefs and practical ideas, even the organization of society itself. These reifications are then received back by the individual to shape his and her own subjective ruling ideas, symbols, and root metaphors, so that they are congruous with those of public life and of everyone else. Only when discord arises between inner and outer is the process itself likely to be laid bare, and questions about the social one and many raised with awkward intensity.

Insofar as this is how things work, the model can help us deal with the history and future of religion; for often religion is precisely the story of those symbols, whether before mind or eye and ear, which above all are supposed to be both public and profoundly internalized. The past, then, becomes a historical sequence of such functioning chains, "mentalities" in the term associated with the French Annales school.[15] Religion's future is merely its future history. One may speak, then, of the Roman mentality, or the mentality of Heian Japan or medieval Europe, and mean by that the working of a definable set of symbols, root images, or metaphors telling what the world is like, and how human life ought to be lived and the social hierarchy set up. These are the symbols displayed outwardly in the contours of temples, courts, and wayside shrines, and inwardly in one's geography of thought.

The catch, of course, is that the chain never spins with unbroken smoothness. One can, of course, find societies and historical moments in which it seems to be working at maximum efficiency, corresponding to what may be called the "classical" expression of a religion or social milieu, when its symbolic potential was best enacted. Yet dissonances that can cause the chain to rattle, and perhaps even break and fly into fragments, are never far away.

They can be of two kinds, external and internal. No society can forever remain insulated from foreign influences, and except for a few extreme cases, such as the Eskimo, not many have been isolated very long or very thoroughly. Yet the presence of outside symbols can only be disturbing to a society's chain. Either they must be assimilated to it, running the risk of overload, or they must be ignored, creating unspoken but dangerous subjective tension.

Internal dissonances arise because, however well programmed, no society can make the lives of all its individuals exactly identical. Personal different experience, personal joys and sorrows and unguarded observations, may well evoke the presence in one's mind of something that doesn't "fit." Much the same options obtain for dealing with these internal goblins as for external incursions. One may try to make a fit however much that means bending and twisting the functioning chain, or one may try to ignore the inconsistencies, but inevitably the chain will never run as evenly as before.

Or in both cases one may take up a third option, to make the new symbol, or the rogue experience, *more* real than the old system. One may then build a new chain based on it for oneself and anyone else one can bring into that fresh new universe. One can become a convert to the outsider's religion, or receive a new revelation from an old (or new) god, or even embrace a foreign faith, but in a novel way conditioned by one's native culture.

Or one may, of course, try a fourth option, rejecting all symbols as equally *un*real; but that is easier said than done.

Three entities, then—symbol (including words and concepts as well as art), society, and the individual—endlessly interact in the flow of historical time. To say which came first is akin to the proverbial chicken-and-egg issue. The "real world" interaction of the three entities is intricate beyond the power of any general theory fully to describe. As in quantum theory, one can at best only suggest probabilities and averages. Two extremes are to be avoided: the Hegelian fallacy of subordinating the individual so much to the dynamics of the history of consciousness that one's significance is no more than that allotted by one's place in the scheme of things entire; and an opposite historical nominalism that would see history as no more than countless individual actions and reactions, without a course that can be plotted by looking at forces immanent in the dominant symbols and ideas of social units themselves.

Our view, so far as the history and future of religions is concerned, is that religious epochs with distinct "mentalities" do exist, and further that they proceed one to another not only in reaction to what is going on in the world, but also through dynamics internal to religious history. In this sense one can speak of an autonomous history of spiritual consciousness.

At the same time, this history need not be seen as determinative of the consciousness of individuals, even of seriously religious individuals, as we have seen in the case of medieval Europe. Dynamics other than the prevailing religious mentality can affect the individual, and do. Different persons may be affected differently by the disruptive factors we have mentioned, external incursion of new symbols and personal dissonant experiences. More mentalities than one may be in the air, and crosswind pressures may be rising within the souls of men and women.

But before taking a further look at the weather vane atop the churches and temples of today, we need to look back to where religion came from and what it may be.

Chapter 2

Religious Origins and Meanings

How did human religion begin? The nineteenth century was much taken with the problem of origins. Not only the origin of religion, but the origin of speech, of species, and of life itself preoccupied savants as they struggled to reorient understanding of the world to conform to empirical methods and Darwinian evolutionary models.

Ultimately, though, the scientific quest for origins was not as far removed as one might think from the romanticism that also tinted the Victorian century. For both scholar and poet, the quest for sunrise origins was a form of renewal of the ancient mythical quest for *meaning* in origins, founded on the assumption that if one knows where something came from, one knows what it really is, and so what it means.

That is the premise behind creation myths around the world. Compare a Vedic account of Prajapati with the creation story according to Genesis. In the Hindu version, the primal being makes the world by dividing up his own body as a great sacrifice; in Genesis, God calls sky, sea, and land into existence as entities outside himself, as though cabinets made by a carpenter. The first narrative tells us that the world *is* God in disguise; to find God we look around and above all within. The second reveals that God is *not* the creation—indeed, to confuse Creator and creature is the supreme blasphemy—but rather the world owes everything to the sovereign will by which it was made, and therefore should reply with gratitude, love, and faithful service. Two paradigms of religious life, and two pictures of ultimate meaning, therefore, are contained in the narrative of origins.

Yet the nineteenth century, in its new empirical quest for origins and its new biological evolution narrative, could only be painfully ambivalent as to meaning. Darwinism presumed movement from the simpler to the more complex. Simple to complex seemed to be the way things worked, not only in biology, but also in cosmology, language, society, religion.

But is this progress? On many levels, from mystical virtue to "elegant" science informed by Occam's razor, simplicity is what is commended. Evolution from the primordial slime to the four-legged and finally the large-brained, the growth of language from grunts to Shakespeare—ordinarily one counts this progress, just as the Darwinian age itself was marked by immense "progress" in both technology and democracy.

Yet it was also possible to idealize instead evolutionary starting points in light of romantic images of the sterling primitive, and to make the time of origins a dawn of forgotten wonder and wisdom. That was the era perhaps of Thoreau's "Bhagvat-Geeta, since whose composition years of the gods have elapsed, and in comparison with which our modern world and its literature seem puny and trivial";[1] for in looking for wisdom, the sage of Walden said elsewhere, "I hear only the resounding of the ancient sea."[2]

But as the century advanced the romantic patina more and more wore off to bare the hard metal of the social Darwinism of Herbert Spencer or Comtean evolutionary positivism. It seemed increasingly clear that the Darwinian meaning better suited those reductionists who wished to say that life was "nothing but" the primal muck decked out in pretentious array, or religion "nothing but" the crude sorcery from which it presumably derived.

Theories of the origin of religion, then, inevitably started with a rude and simple, one-dimensional original, from which faith proceeded step by step to "higher" levels. The anthropologist John Lubbock (1834–1913), in *The Origin of Civilization and the Primitive Condition of Man,* proposed a pattern of religious evolution commencing with the absence of religion, and proceeding through "fetishism," nature worship, totemism, shamanism, anthropomorphism, monotheism, and ethical monotheism. Edward B. Tylor (1832–1917), the great pioneer ethnologist, hypothesized that religion started in animism, a belief in souls separable from the body first suggested by the experience of dreams, in which one apparently left one's body during sleep to travel to far places and even meet persons deceased on the plane of waking life. From this it was easy to extrapolate the existence of souls in other entities, animals, the moving wind and sun, and to elaborate doctrines of ancestrism and the afterlife. A further short step led to polytheism, and then a long one to monotheism, in which all these powers are brought under a single rule with ethical consequences.

However, Andrew Lang (1844–1912), the distinguished Scottish folklorist, was disturbed by ethnological reports from the field that, contrary to animist theory, told of belief among some of the technologically most undeveloped peoples in a quasi-monotheistic "high god." He proposed a primal monotheism, whose deity was Creator and often moral legislator. Critics, however, were quick to point out that this figure was frequently a *deus otiosus,* an inactive divine shadow in the background who did not really interfere with the prevailing evolutionary schema. Nonetheless, Wilhelm Schmidt (1868–1964), a German-Austrian priest and anthropologist, enthusiastically took up the cause of *Urmonotheismus* and published voluminously in its support.

R. R. Marett (1866–1943), an English anthropologist critical of both Tylor and Lang, traced religion back past animist to a "preanimist" stage of "animatism," the veneration, or rather generation through dance or feelings of awe, of sheer impersonal, supernatural power, the energy known by such names as *mana* or *wakan.* Sir James Frazer (1854–1941), in his much-cited *The Golden Bough,* put magic in first place, contending that primitives worked sorcery before they conceived of gods, turning to the propitiation of personal deities only when they found that magic did not consistently succeed. The great popularity of Frazer's writings, despite the lack of real empirical support for this hypothesis, is a tribute to his elegant, if often condescending, presentation of religious lore from around the world, and to the sovereign power of the simple-to-complex evolutionary model.

In the early twentieth century, the search for a primordial simplicity by which to interpret the origin of religion persisted, though with psychological perspectives tending to displace anthropological ones. Lucien Lévy-Bruhl spoke of "primitive mentality" as an associational way of thinking in which certain cause-

and-effect relations could be overlooked in favor of magical sorts of symbolic connections. Émile Durkheim emphasized the societal origins of religion in the "social effervescence" of a tribe or group in dance or festival; like many nineteenth-century scholars, he gave great importance to the totem as a sacrament of tribal unity.

The centrality of totemism was taken up by the father of psychoanalysis, Sigmund Freud, who viewed it as the relic of the unspeakable crime that religion atones for: the primal patricide. On the other hand, Jungian thinkers such as Erich Neumann put at the beginning an undifferentiated consciousness, the "ouroboros," which gradually divides itself up into various archetypes that are the stuff of gods and goddesses. Other thinkers, more strictly in the history of religions tradition, seemed to put the beginning of religion in a single psychic capacity. For G. van der Leeuw it was the quest for "power"; for Rudolf Otto a sense of the "numinous," that which is "Wholly Other" and a *mysterium tremendens et fascinans.*

But it was becoming increasingly clear that explanations on the order of these, which strove to reduce religion to some single transparent source, would at best never be more than partial. They did not really deal with all the complexity that is religion. They continually gave one a feeling of trying to cover a jagged parcel with a wrapping that never quite fits; when one corner is well enveloped it slips somewhere else, leaving a whole side exposed to the light.

So then it seemed that we needed to set aside the quest for origins and simply understand more deeply what religion is. That was the midcentury task of structuralism and its allies in the phenomenological study of religion. The fashionable labors of Claude Lévi-Strauss stressed the importance of polarities in thinking, providing tools for the understanding of ritual versus ordinary behavior, the meaning of culture, and the analysis of myth. The more religiously sensitive scholarship of Mircea Eliade emphasized the dialectic of the sacred and the profane, and the countless manifestations the sacred can take. His work served well to bridge the gulf between the romantic and the reductionist; in it, the sacred and profane may change expression as they move from the primordial to the modern, but the fundamental dialectic remains; even among contemporaries hidden remnants of the holy linger.

A final stage, to date, seems to be the "deconstructionism" of Jacques Derrida and the related "postmodernism" of writers such as Jean-François Lyotard and Richard Rorty. These commentators are bound to have an increasing impact on the history of religions. Their movements may be summarized under two agendas: they criticize the "modern" approach, which sees history as a "Grand Narrative" or "metanarrative" of progress from myth and mystification to enlightenment and rationality; and they try to show that any quest for language freed from metaphor, and therefore innocent of any incipient mythicization submerging particulars under a grand scheme, is destined to fail.

Jean-François Lyotard has identified the two great reigning metanarratives (or myths, in religious language) as, first, the emancipation of humanity by progress, both political and scientific; and, second, the unity of knowledge in a way amenable to rational, "scientific" abstraction and technological implementation.[3] On these premises the modern university is built, and on the other hand any "knowledge" not reducible to their categories is marginalized or excluded, for the most part not even seen. Lyotard writes that "modern" designates "any science that legitimates itself with reference to a metadiscourse of this kind [essentially the enlightenment and emancipation narratives by which science interprets its career] making an explicit appeal to some grand narrative, such as the dialectics of Spirit, the hermeneutics of meaning, the emancipation of the rational or working subject, or the creation of wealth."[4] We are, however, moving past this level of perception: "Simplifying to the extreme, I define *postmodern* as incredulity toward metanarratives. . . . This incredulity is undoubtedly a product of progress in the sciences; but that progress in turn presupposes it."[5] Science continually bursts fables, including—most painfully—its own. We have seen that religion also builds and breaks mythicizations of its own history, whether triumphalist or secularizationist.

Postmodernism proceeds to postulate that a purely rational language unifying all truth, mythless and metaphorless, has not been shown possible, and the modern illusion that modern observers have a privileged line of vision that sets them apart from their medieval or earlier counterparts is an idolatry of the present we must get beyond. Historians of religion, for all their honest endeavors to recover empathetically the spiritual past, have not always been free, in the last analysis, of presuming to do so from the uniquely high ground of the "modern" age. Obviously, the "myth of modernity" was egregiously represented, not only by the likes of Comte, Marx, or Spencer, but also by the origin of religion theorists we have noted, with their neat progressions from naive beginnings through fetishism, polytheism, and the like to a modern high point, whether "ethical monotheism" or the transcendence of religion altogether.

The postmodern critique has not pleased everyone. Lyotard's great philosophical antagonist, Jürgen Habermas, has asked, "But where are the works which might fill the negative slogan of 'postmodernism' with a positive content?"[6] The point is well taken that postmodernism, like deconstructionism, seems satisfied merely with dismantling the great edifices of modernity in the mind, regardless of whether their wrecking ball leaves only a wasteland. To some extent Habermas himself shares that project; he talks of the way historical or scientific narratives leave "subtexts," matters about which they are silent, under their flow of words—the lives of the past human multitudes who did not "make history" as the Grand Narratives understand it, the orphan truths that do not fit into the current scientific unified view. Yet fundamentally Habermas accepts the enlightenment ideal of knowledge that, fully known and freely communicated, will emancipate. Failure to accept such knowledge even as an ideal, he believes, leaves the postmodern camp merely negative, liable to fall for either bleak pessimism or some neoconservative nostrum.

Others might feel it is precisely liberation from abstract goals and ideals that leaves one truly free and effective. One is now free to enjoy the art and wisdom of all times and places without chronological comparison, and one is free to do what needs to be done to meet human need directly without mystification by politics or ideology. To be sure, several layers of self-deception can obtain in the quest for this kind of freedom before it is authentically actualized. For some, deconstruction and postmodernism have led to a Heideggerean, or Zen, kind of voiceless awareness of things as they appear, and action-needs as they are performed, in all their concreteness, without myth or theory. If in the process one rejects as discredited the modern rational outlook, including its liberal religious and social agendas, that need not require the compensatory purchase of some conservative or other myth. Perhaps once could optimistically hold, with William LaFleur, that "the problem is not that emancipation is unreal or not worth searching and fighting for—although some post-modernists may have gone to that conclusion. Rather it is that emancipation is real and recognizable enough to be able to do without the grand old metanarratives of modernity. It also is something that can be encouraged and forced by the concerned—without the need for some kind of belief in the possibility of getting a language 'freed' of metaphor."[7]

That conclusion would, more than coincidentally, be supported by much of the more sophisticated of recent historiography, whether Herman Ooms's *Tokugawa Ideology* (from the review of which the above passage by LaFleur is taken) or the harvest of the Annales school of social history, such as Le Roy Ladurie's *Montaillou*. Scholars such as these have convincingly shown that the situation vis-à-vis myth and reason and times past was by no means as clear-cut as the metanarratives of modern "enlightenment" would have had it.

Either way, the implications of deconstruction and postmodernism for the history of religions are profound. They may succeed in demolishing that discipline altogether, showing it to be a project hopelessly bound to modernism. They may leave in its place only a nihilism and a conviction that—at least on the level of its vaunted role as a "new humanism" able to achieve "phenomenological empathy" and "intuit essences" with faith across the ages—the history of religions absurdly overabsolutized its own standpoint. To the contrary, historical minimalists may urge, nothing can be known, especially of the religious past; or if it can, it can only be intuited subjectively but not communicated in words; or if words are used, they can only point to the scattered outer husks of faith, not to any essence or splendid story.

Nonetheless, our position is that a history of religions founded on a concept of stages of spiritual mentalities is possible. Ideally, this would not be a history subject to any metanarrative, but a history of reigning metanarratives themselves. It would thus take the demolishers of metanarratives at their word, allowing them to set the historiographical agenda, for if metanarratives are more than mere bogeymen—or even if they are—they must themselves have a history and one not far distanced from the history of religion.

This history would be the story of the myths and metaphors, illusory or not, that have dominated the historical development of religions. Not all persons have had equal relations to them, but they have affected the great religious institutions, and usually political institutions as well. In order to remain independent of any "modern" or other tale, this history ought to take each religious era as its own center of meaning, in the sense of Wilhelm Dilthey,[8] emphasizing the internal dynamics of religious development rather than the role of religions as parts of a larger world process.

In this perspective, the question of the origin of religion is the wrong question, for it assumes the evolutionary simple-to-complex story upon which the modernist stance was built. Indeed, when a question proves itself as intractable as has this one, we can be confident that it is somehow not being put right. We must recognize that, just as we cannot locate for sure any "prereligious" human society past or present, so we cannot pinpoint any particular principle or experience as where it all began.

Rather, the development of human religion is clearly coeval with the development of two profoundly interrelated faculties—thought and language. We must note that religion simply runs in the channels of human thought itself, in that it provides categories by which to divide up the world into ours and theirs, right and wrong, dangerous and useful, good feelings and bad. Religion provides exemplars for the correct and incorrect way to do things, for what communicates coinherence with other humans and what does not, for what gives one power and what weakens one. The transmission of such distinctions is perhaps initially through enactments and, soon, stories about ideal types—the great hunter or warrior or mother. But quickly and without fuss the models become ontological, for religion inevitably sets the truly real against the only apparently real, affirming that the latter cannot properly "work." Early religion requires no metaphysical subtlety to assume tacitly that the ritual gestures that really work are aligned with the inner forces that keep the universe going, or that the archetypal hunter has a sort of aseity and hunting omniscience.

These images in the mind are no more than parts of human speech and therefore of human verbalized thought, for they are what speech is all about. What is there to talk about except to make such contrasts as between right and wrong ways of hunting or socializing or between good and bad feelings? And to establish one's identity in terms of these contrasts and the various situations life presents? It is a question, however, of *how* contrasts and personal identities are talked about, with what referential signposts. Here is where the inseparability of thought, language, and metaphor shows itself. For how can one talk about, say, right and wrong behavior without story, without example in which the part stands for the whole, and the concrete for the abstract, prior to the appearance of the generic language that can only come after stories and concrete examples, since it generalizes from them? Two sources for such metaphor-making referents present themselves.

One is the capacity for proto-language and proto-religious behavior *already* embedded in the human psyche, having been carried over from the animal kingdom. Before the human dawn, our animal ancestors already bore a fairly complete set of "religious" gestures, ready to have bestowed on them the gift of speech to make them vehicles for behavior testing and ontological reification. One thinks of the ritualized activity by which certain species define territory and inaugurate mating, or the responses—often highly symbolic—by which animals deal with danger, rivalry, and the presence of food or water. The playful running and scuffling of young animals imitating adult behavior suggests not only the festive play of religious life, but also religion's ritual imitation of "real life" activities—the hunt or the communal meal—under controlled conditions to enact their ideal form and inner meaning. A more poignant note is offered by the obvious sorrow that primates, at least, can show for the death of a child or mate, and the altruism of members of primate bands who, in well-documented instances, have given their lives for the sake of the rest.

All these are clearly feelings and actions that, given speech, would easily describe and enact themselves through story, itself half acted out as it would be by any good storyteller or audience. The story in turn perpetuates the act or attitude, making it and its protagonists part of a timelessly available firmament of referents. The hunter or bereaved one or self-sacrificer becomes a hero or god or the reflection of one here below; the play-ritual time and place are, in the Australian term, the dreamtime of ultimate origin and power.

The second source of metaphor-making referents is the meta-phorical material at hand. The fundamental religious images are cosmic: light and dark, high and low, center and periphery, cause and effect. They are always there, waiting to be internalized and then revalorized as virtue and sin, gods and demons. Thus religion can provide a language, a vocabulary and grammar, for talking about contrasts and coordinating them with cosmic good and bad, right and wrong, positive and negative.

What kind of language would be religious? The definition of religion is a notoriously thorny problem, and the difficulty probably tells us that, as in the case of the origin of religion, the definitional question is the wrong, or at least a highly artificial, way to put the issue. For although we may be talking about where what we call religion came from, to think of our early ancestors' gestures and acted stories as their "religion" is anachronistic by hundreds of thousands, perhaps millions, of years.

People were doing and saying things we might label religious long before any such word or concept obtained. As William Cant-well Smith has shown, words and concepts for religion in the modern sense, as a clear and distinct area of human life having to do with faith in the supernatural, are a modern creation in the major languages.[9] Traditional terms, such as Dharma, Tao or Tō, and Islam, embrace the social order, a proper way of life for an individual, and the sacred cosmos that is its largest context; these are an inseparable, seamless whole. All the more, in that long-forgotten human daybreak when speech was being forged, would any distinction of religious and secular speech be vacant.

To name someone a god or hero would be no different from assigning him a role; to hold to a kinship between a tribe and an animal or sacred stone or mountain would be no different from naming the tribe and knowing its place and its unity, though the kinship might be portrayed in art, cemented with offerings, and enacted in dance; to say that such behavior is in accord with the ways of the ancestors or the dreamtime is no different from saying it is right, though the right ways may be enforced through the sense of mysterious dread that talk of ancient ones and other-ness can instill. But the point is that to use such language, lan-guage labeled by us religious, is no special thing save in terms of our own "modern" metanarrative, which makes religion a sepa-rate, detachable part of human experience, and one at odds with

Shaman with reindeer horns and drum. Tungus Tribe (Siberia). Reprinted from S. Giedion, *The Eternal Present: The Beginnings of Art.* Bollingen Series XXXV.6.I (New York: Pantheon Books, 1962), illus. 339.

"modern" enlightenment and rationality. At the dawn of speech religious talk was neither peculiarly exalted nor Max Müller's "disease of language"; it was simply a way of speech that was at hand, inbred in already-present animal-human moods and rituals, waiting to be given names that both made important distinctions and enforced them, while connecting humankind to the cosmic environment.

What it comes down to is a manipulation of images. Although perhaps no definitive statement can ever be made here, it seems likely that the emergence of images in consciousness as distinct entities with which one could have varied and considered relationships, rather than as blurs of sense impressions or stimuli evoking only conditioned or instinctual responses, was coeval with language. Language offered tools for the separation of one image from another, for retention of distinct images in memory, and for constructing the grammar of rational response to them in the mind. It also afforded the communication of images, which makes them social as well as private entities.

Images are of three orders. First are the images created in the mind by sensory data, whether from the cosmic environment or one's own body—the images making conscious what is seen, heard, felt. These become clear, retained images insofar as one gives each a separate character and stores it in memory for future reference.

Second are the images both outward and subjective created by art or voice, also of course communicated through the senses but very different in that they are known to mediate a human, socially significant meaning and are retained for the hopes and fears they evoke concerning one's relation to society as well as the cosmos.

Third are those images that exist only in subjectivity: dreams, fantasies, visualized cogitations.

In addition, intermediate categories linking two or three of these orders exist: remembrance (accurate or otherwise), or known facts and abstract ideas that may well be carried in the mind under some sort of image. As Owen Barfield has commented, abstractions are but decayed metaphors.[10]

Religion, of course, may plant itself in any of the three orders. Explicitly religious images, in the sense of altars or gods or other symbols of transcendent reality, may be seen "naturally" in the outer world, be created by art, or arise in the subjective consciousness. But the great function of religion is that it connects these orders, providing vehicles for bridging barriers between them and thus overcoming the isolation of subjectivity from the world, or of the human from the natural. Gods within may be fashioned of wood or stone and may be imputed to rule over sky and sea; the forms of natural power, such as sun, moon, or wind, are given meaning compatible with human subjectivity. Peter Berger has written that "religion is man's audacious attempt to see the whole universe as humanly significant";[11] that is certainly at least one side of the truth about religion, one that points to its close affinity to language.

Language is also that which connects meaning to meaning, inner to outer and outer to inner, humanizing the cosmos insofar as it names it, though not to the extent of religion when it both names and personifies the cosmos or the power behind it. Nonetheless, we again see religion as a form of language, or perhaps more profoundly see language as a form of religion. On different levels of intensity and personification, both define and interpret the images in their orders, connecting human subject and cosmic object.

To pursue further the matter of the origin of religion, we need now to look at the origin of humans in more precise anthropological terms. When did humans become human? Paleoanthropologists speak of hominid species in the evolutionary chain leading to modern man as *Pithecus* and *Homo,* ape and man. Characteristic of the protohuman *Pithecus* stage is *Australopithecus afarensis* of some four million years back; one star of the *A. afarensis* set is "Lucy," discovered and described by Donald Johnson.[12]

The evolutionary transition to the protohuman state represented by Lucy, who walked more or less upright, was gradual and marked by three early characteristics: bipedalism, brain development, and use of tools. At one time it was thought that these three more or less emerged together. But the discovery of the small-brained, toolless but bipedal Lucy and her kin pushed bipedalism back a million years and, in the eyes of many authorities, made evident its priority over the other two features.

Why was bipedalism the *first* major step toward true humanity, the one upon which the growth of a large brain and the use of tools apparently depended? The answer may have intriguing connections with the question of religion.

Nonbipedal primates use two main means of locomotion: they are branch swingers or knuckle walkers. Another important feature of most nonhuman primates is a low birthrate. Females generally raise only one child at a time, spacing them over several years, and have only occasional estrus; when this occurs the males in the local band become highly aroused, fighting in a general free-for-all for the privilege of mating with her. These chaotic arrangements are largely responsible for the low numbers and poor prospects of most primates in the world, despite their intelligence and, in some ways, elaborate social organization. The low birthrate makes survival an always-precarious affair, and the sexual infighting inhibits social evolution by periodically disrupting cooperation and harmony.

C. Owen Lovejoy has suggested that one branch of the primate family, the protohuman, found its way out of this box. It prospered sexually and socially through three interrelated evolutionary developments: bipedalism, the pair bonding of one male and one female, and continuous sexual contact resulting in much more frequent births.[13]

Bipedalism was the key. This new mode of movement meant, first, that a female with a child was relatively tied to one place—home—since a bipedal child does not cling to its mother like a monkey but is carried in her arms. The male, on the other hand, is free to walk out and find food and has free arms with which to bring it back. The prospect of sex, as well as emotional bonding to mate and offspring, motivated him to return with provender, and this increased the birthrate. These interconnected adaptations, according to Lovejoy's ingenious theory, developed over millions of years and led up to *Australopithecus* and finally *Homo*.

All this probably took place in the context of climate changes in Africa, man's first home, some four to five million years ago, when drying changed much of the continent from forest to savanna. That doubtless increased the value of bipedalism by making our distant ancestors taller and thus able to spot food or predators farther away, and strengthening mobility in open terrain. Like Lucy and her folk, they probably ranged in family groups or small bands in the vicinity of lakes and streams, gathering and foraging.

The next stage was the emergence of *Homo habilis* and *Homo erectus,* early man, still short of *Homo sapiens,* contemporary man, beginning some two million years ago. Now hunting, and the associated making of bladelike tools, became important. This in turn probably meant socially the formation of male bands who continued the ancient work of bringing home food, but now often by means of cooperative quests for game. The cooperation needed for bringing down and preparing large animals undoubtedly facilitated human social development, and the manufacture of tools for killing and dressing the prey encouraged technological advance. All this went hand in hand with mental expansion—the coming of the large brain.

And religion? According to conventional theology, protohumans would have become *homo* upon being infused with a soul, an immortal spiritual part distinct from body and mind, capable of knowing God and in acute interaction with supersensory reality. We have absolutely no way of knowing how Lucy and her folk thought, much less whether she knew God, nor have we any better idea of the real status of thought or God for *Homo erectus* a couple of million years later.

But if the foregoing hypotheses are correct, we can well imagine some sort of sanctions in the mind enforcing pair bonding, the nurture of children, and the loyalty of hunting bands. They may also have dealt with emergent feelings of joy and grief. Inner sanctions must have arisen simultaneously with the outer social and emotional developments, and taken verbalized form much later as language appeared, reinforced with conceptualized mental images. Images must have linked subjective consciousness and outer social need through words as soon as language itself presented that intangible tool kit. For, again, these are what the linkages and distinctions language makes are all about.

We ourselves know all too well that our first impulses are not always in the direction of loyalty to mate and community good; we need not think our remote ancestors were any different. The crucial areas of family and tribal bonding, of sexual control and subordination of self to hunting and work group, of altruism to the point of self-sacrifice when necessary—still underneath all else the vital arenas of religious sanction—must have required some inner, as well as social, discipline capable of overriding "natural" impulse when need be. The symbols used could only be those which, by sign or metaphor, by the image linkages made, indicated a dimension within which human life operated other than the ordinary outward, visible, and natural.

The sociobiologist Edward Wilson has persuasively argued the superior survival value of communalism and, within the community, of the inculcation of altruism. Among verbal creatures, he further argues, religion is the supreme vehicle for this stern but necessary teaching.[14] The fundamental sociobiological point is that human behavior, including worship and morality, ultimately derive from biological natural selection designed to assure group and species survival.

As a full explanation of religion, this case may be one-sided; in my view, at least, religion has probably always answered to a human capacity for poetic vision and yearning for ultimate understanding, as well as provided sanctions for behavior with species survival value, including loyalty and altruistic self-sacrifice. Sociobiology, in fact, presents a first-class example of a metanarrative rank with subtexts about the privileged position of the scientific observer and progress toward enlightenment and emancipation. Like so many other metanarratives, it is finally undercut by its inability to explain itself in a way congruous with the way it explains everything else. If sociobiology can explain religion, and the rest of human society, merely as ploys wrought by the cunning of the gene, where did sociobiology itself come from? How do we know it is not also just another plausible myth, foisted on us for some survival value our masters deep within the cells have decided it holds, though it is really no more true than any other fable? Perhaps some evolutionary *élan vital* is now shifting its human bets from religion to science, assuming—an awesome assumption—that science now holds the greater survival value and is implanting the appropriate tales. But does that make them *true?*

These issues are, however, something of a digression from our investigation of the origin of religion. We do not doubt that a major function of the earliest human religion—whatever else it may have been—was to offer necessary sanctions as part of its role as a language making distinctions between good and bad, or ours and theirs. A basic problem with Wilson, as with all spokespersons for the scientific narrative of the rational unity of knowledge and the narrative of modern emancipation from myth, is their inability to countenance fully that early religion, like language, may have truly had more than one "origin," insofar as it served more than one end, and that it was not (as it appears to emancipated moderns) a well-defined, detachable, and therefore dispensable segment of human life.

But if what we call religion began as language linking inner and outer images, the point is that it was really nothing special and therefore nothing about which dispensability as an issue would arise. It was a way of thinking, a vocabulary, for dealing with essential commitments and necessities of human social life—and perhaps increasingly, for maintaining inner equilibrium in the face of fear, the need for deferred reward, and the inevitable tension created by conflicting obligations. The question of whether it was the *best* language would not arise until language has advanced, or decayed, sufficiently to produce abstract as well as personified metaphors, and so allow a choice between them. Then, finally, some decision between the "religious" and the "philosophical" ways of handling such matters was available. From the beginning, however, no doubt varying degrees of emotional relation to religious images was found.

At some point, we know not when, humanity made the ultimate discovery: death. Avoidance of death—or seeking it whether for altruistic or suicidal reasons—was then not merely based on instinctual fear, but compounded by conscious awareness of what death was, and extrapolation from the sight of death in others. Death, too, came under the canopy of religious language, for death above all had to be dealt with in a way fusing inner feelings and their images with outer, observed realities.

Primal religion was then a way of thinking and talking about such things, unselfconscious in its use of symbol and metaphor as tools of language. That is nothing remarkable, for that use was not discontinuous with the symbolic character of all language and acts, human or animal, in the context of social relations that say what is not fully done at the moment, or is to be completed in subjectivity, from the raised fist and the stroking gesture to the courtship dance.

Early true humans, *Homo erectus,* move onstage a million or so years ago. *Homo erectus* was, in all likelihood, responsible for several immensely important steps in human development: the dispersion of the race outside Africa, the taming of fire, cooking of food, cave dwelling. Did they also move ahead in religion? Most sites leave nothing that seems susceptible of a religious explanation—no burials, no sacred art, nothing but the most severely utilitarian hearths and stone tools. This does not, of course, mean there was nothing, for what has survived so many thousands of years can only represent a tiny percentage of *Homo erectus's* total culture. Whatever was made of sand, wood, or skin, not to mention all the songs and all the stories insofar as they communicated in human sound, is forever lost. Nonetheless, in the absence of any positive evidence to the contrary, we must conclude that *Homo erectus* had not yet found the capacity to express subjectivity in the symbolic forms of art, although—since animal parallels exist—we may well hypothesize such articulation through voice and gesture, and even dance.

The most oft-cited evidence of religious practice by *Homo erectus* involves two of the grimmest activities in religion's repertoire: headhunting and cannibalism. These are particularly associated with the remains found at Chou Kou-Tien in North China ("Peking Man"). Here human bones have been broken and splintered as though to eat the marrow, and skulls are detached from bodies and collected. Further, the skulls show damage at the base of the cranium in a way that would allow the brain to be extracted; recent headhunters of Borneo and New Guinea have ritually removed the brain of a victim in a similar manner and eaten it as a way of assuming the deceased's name and identity.

Some authorities, however, have questioned the headhunting and cannibalism interpretations of such *Homo erectus* finds, pointing out that in all known recent cultures such practices are inevitably associated with Neolithic (archaic agricultural) societies rather than the most primitive. Maringer, for example, has held that the evidence would also be compatible with a far more benign explanation, the practice of some of the most primitive peoples on earth, such as the Andaman Islanders, of removing, cleaning, and carrying about with them the heads of departed loved ones as tokens of remembrance and vessels of their protective power.[15]

Either way, we need not doubt that these earliest hints of some kind of ritual activity with the heads and bones of the dead of their own kind had a connection with that dreadful discovery already mentioned. In some vague but powerful way, perhaps, *Homo erectus* sensed a lingering—or enhanced—invisible energy in the dead, which could be appropriated by the living, doubtless directly or indirectly to challenge their own deaths, in rites by which one symbolically faced and mastered the last enemy.

It was during the fourth, or Würm, glaciation some 75,000 years ago that Neanderthal, an early *Homo sapiens,* appeared. With him came the first unambiguous evidence of religious life. In both Europe and the Middle East, this powerfully built race attained the highest level of culture known thus far. The Neanderthals provide the first clear instance of intentional burial, with the remains treated in a way unmistakably significant: smeared with ochre, the color of blood and life; the burial of family groups together; the placing of new tools and pieces of meat in the grave with the deceased. The most remarkable Neanderthal burial is at Shanidar in eastern Iraq. Here some 60,000 years ago a man was laid to rest, fossilized pollen tells us, on a bed of diverse flowers of many colors: hyancinth, mallow, hollyhock, bachelor's button, groundsel. A further discovery provides more insight into Neanderthal culture: prior to death, this beautifully buried man had lost the use of one eye and his right arm, showing that despite severe handicaps he was not only kept alive by his people, but considered important enough to warrant splendid obsequies. One hypothesis is that he may have been a shaman.

Neanderthal religion was not restricted to human burial rites; purposefully placed skulls suggest a bear cult such as has been practiced by circumpolar peoples down to the present, in which the remains of that mighty adversary become guardians of home and hearth. Yet, again, what remains we have indicate that above all it was the mysterious threshold between life and death that focused spiritual imagination. The symbols of life—blood and flowers—go with the departed on their strange journey; the residual power of the dead, whether man or beast, remain with the living to bless, or perhaps curse, their kin.

The next great stage appears with Cro-Magnon man some 35,000 years ago; he is the first human virtually indistinguishable from present-day folk in appearance, in use of language (many believe), and, it would seem, in intellect. The Cro-Magnons are celebrated above all for their famous cave paintings, the first major works of art and of undoubted, though enigmatic, religious significance.

These illustrations were not mere picture galleries, nor the

decorations of homes. They are in sanctuaries obviously reserved
for sacred activities, located far underground away from living
areas, accessible then as now only by arduous and dangerous
journeys through narrow passageways. After such a subterranean
trek, the light of the Cro-Magnon's torch would fall on the bright
colors of game animals painted on the walls and even ceilings of a
hidden inner chamber, animals painted over and over, often one
superimposed on another.

We can only imagine what those familiar yet mysterious forms
would have meant to those who saw them freshly hued. No doubt
one purpose had to do with hunting magic. By painting and
probably ritually slaying the underground animals, their counterparts in field and forest might also be made susceptible to the
tribesmen's spears. But the meaning may go beyond this. It is not
unlikely the caves were places of initiation. In one, footprints in a
room by the gallery recall the stomping or dancing of many
childish feet before the last ice age; they may well derive from an
initiatory scenario.

John E. Pfeiffer, in *The Creative Explosion: An Inquiry into the
Origins of Art and Religion,* has proposed another possible meaning
of cave art, suggested by patterns in more contemporary Australian and San (Bushman) rock paintings—that they are aids to
mythic memory and storehouses of tribal wisdom.[16] However
chaotic the dense packs of cave pictures may seem to the modern
observer, the stylized formats and the arrangements of the paintings in particular caves may tell stories important to the people
responsible for them, encoding events from mythology, history,
and festivals, and perhaps also mapping sacred geography. (Aus-
tralians, for example, learned and remembered the lay of their
land through stories of mythic events believed to have taken place
at various important sites.) Since it is customarily in initiatory
ceremonies that such secret and sacred lore is imparted, it would
not be surprising if meanings like these were contained in the art
ornamenting the scene of cave initiations.

Now we clearly see the rebounding reflections of the image so
characteristic of human society. In the picture caves we find that
which had been seen in nature, and perhaps also in dreams and
visions, reconstructed in art. Thereby, first, its human meaning, as
possible tokens recalling myth and geographical orientation, is
revealed; and, second, its magico-sacred meaning, as instruments

of power and initiation now. Perhaps the Cro-Magnon caves, like so many later caves, were portals to the Other World, associated with gods and the dead. In any case, the full-fledged discovery of art they symbolize surely opened countless Gates of Horn to true dreaming both sacred and profane, unveiling ranges of human self-awareness and cosmic awareness heretofore sealed off.

Another feature of archaic religion that unquestionably also exposed fresh frontiers of human subjectivity and sacred consciousness was shamanism. How far back shamanism goes is not entirely clear, but it may well have been associated with the Cro-Magnon caves and their culture. Many have assumed that the famous human figure dressed in animal skins and horns of the Trois-Frères Cave in France, known as the sorcerer and possibly some 12,000 years old, is shamanistic. As we have seen, the far older personage of the Neanderthal floral funeral has also been thought to be a shaman. All that can be said for certain, though, is that shamanism appears to be among the oldest strata of spirituality that the history of religion can trace, well established in many recent tribal societies upon European contact, and offering innumerable clues of its presence in the deep background of the literate religions as they moved into history.

What is shamanism? The term refers to the role of specialists in the sacred who possess direct control of or partnership with spirits and access to the Other World of gods and the departed, and are thereby able to heal and divine. Mircea Eliade, in his classic work *Shamanism: Archaic Techniques of Ecstasy,* offers a vivid and richly documented account of the shaman's call from the gods, "initiatory psychopathology," expanded awareness and vocabulary, role as psychopomp, and capacity for "earth-diving" or marvelous flight.[17] Claude Lévi-Strauss has vividly shown how shamans heal, first, through diagnosis that interprets the cause of illness or misfortune in terms of the society's world view—that is, a lost or stolen soul, invasion by evil spirits, violation of a taboo—which makes it understandable and therefore manageable; and, second, through correcting the dysfunction in the same terms by acting out the recovery of the soul, driving out the malignant entity, atoning for the taboo breakage.[18] Shamanism can be seen as virtuoso handling of religion as a language linking subjective images and cosmic/physical realities; it dramatically and forcefully compels their convergence through spectacular symbols and consciousness-altering "techniques of ecstasy." This is nothing more nor less, of course, than what culture does through all sorts of media. The archaic shaman may rightly be considered the spiritual ancestor of various later religious specialists (the prophet, priest, mystic, and heaven-faring savior); and of various other specialists as well (the artist, poet, singer, and psychotherapist).

Not all shamans in all societies have played all the roles we have cited. But in all genuine cases images of that which is more than biological, and aligned to the realm of dream and vision, break through in the shaman. In him or her the human, and the god who personifies that other realm, become visibly linked as co-workers and mutual visitants, even become identical if the shaman is possessed and acquires, as often happens, the visage and personality of the deity. Both the human and divine are enhanced through the shaman's mediation. The range of human experience is vastly, one might even say infinitely, expanded by the capacity to contain godhead; and the divine, by taking on entranced human face and form, becomes familiar and gains the attributes that may be transmitted down through the centuries in art and song.

After the world of the Paleolithic hunter came that of the Neolithic archaic agriculturalist. With the invention of agriculture came a profound social and religious revolution, one that shaped the nature of human practical and spiritual life more than any other factor down virtually to the present. The city is no more than an extension of the sedentary village made possible by planting; and until the twentieth century the average person almost anywhere in the world was a peasant whose values and way of life was closer to that of the Neolithic farmer than of the contemporary computer programmer. It may be that now, some 12,000 years after the discovery of agriculture, conditions of human life are changing radically enough to suggest religious change as far-reaching as that which separated the Paleolithic hunter and the Neolithic farmer.

What were those changes? First, we may cite those that affected the connection of inner and outer images, the latter now grounded significantly if not directly in nature, but in nature as modified by the human hand. Neolithic religion gives renewed importance to the earth, frequently personified as feminine—Mother Earth—and to feminine fertility symbols in general. The turn of the seasons, with anxious prayers at seedtime and joyful thanksgiving as the harvest is gathered in, punctuate the sacred year. The sedentary nature of agriculture makes especially important permanent sites of the sacred: the holy mountain overlooking the fields, the altar in their midst. A darker dimension of the sacred comes to the fore as well, for the discovery of agriculture seems to have brought with it a new sense of the relation of death and life; a seeming death, like that of the seed buried in the soil, or an actual death, like that of a victim who fertilizes it, can bring abundant life to many in the end. It was in the Neolithic period, not before, that practices such as animal and human sacrifice and headhunting most flourished.

Socially, the Neolithic revolution not only changed the pattern of human life for most by making it stationary, but also produced typically enough surplus wealth and energy, despite great population growth, to make possible homes, granaries, and public buildings such as temples on an unprecedented scale, and to permit at least a small number of people to pursue public roles as rulers, merchants, priests, and even philosophers rather than directly engaging in production. For better or worse, religion, like the statecraft with which it was closely intertwined, was professionalized.

Together that elite of rulers, priests, and merchants living on the surplus produced the next great political-spiritual event—the ancient empires, with their sacred kings and elaborate national cultus and busy commerce affording broad intercultural contacts. These three also pioneered the invention of writing, with all its immense consequences down through the centuries.

It was in the world of the ancient empires and their peripheries, a world whose soul was still profoundly ruled by shamanistic and Neolithic values, but that now knew also the power of the written word to chronicle and consolidate, a world shaken by new discoveries and new terrors, that the next powerful epoch in religion appeared—the Great Religions. Their rising was itself a great moment in religious history, and our religious era still belongs to them. Yet is must be seen that they themselves are but the final, culminating stage of the religious revolution wrought by the discovery of agriculture.

That last stage was marked by a tremendous event, the discovery of history. To it and its meaning we must now turn.

Chapter 3

Religion and the
Discovery of History

How did religion get from its primordial focus on the timeless symbols represented by nature and the human self—the animal, the plant, the soul surviving death—to the focus of the historic Great Religions on the archetypal person, generally the founder, and the single, pivotal historical moment? Continuities there may be, but impressive also is the distance between the cave painting of Trois-Frères or the archaic open-air Shinto shrine facing a sacred mountain or waterfall, to an altar bearing the image of Christ crucified or the Buddha in meditation. No less momentous is the gulf between those faiths whose calendar revolves around seed-time and harvest, and those that celebrate a second creation in Wesak—the day of the Buddha's birth and enlightenment—or Christmas and Easter.

Before proceeding to these reflections, let us review again our understanding of the meaning of religion. Religion is fundamentally a manipulation of images. Above all it establishes connections between three great orders of images: those created by sensory data from the outside world, those humanly created in art and manufacture, and those from the worlds of dream and fantasy and cognition, which—though perhaps inspired by outside forms—truly exist only in subjectivity. As a kind of language, religion connects these realms, saying that the wind or sun are akin to powers or dominions within, and so may be personified in art and ritual, or that gods of the cosmos affect one's dreams and visions. Some authorities believe that true human speech came late, certainly only with *Homo sapiens,* perhaps only with Cro-Magnon man. But if so, the same connections might have been felt, and articulated through sign and gesture rooted in animal sound and ritualism long before. The history of religion is a history of these connections, especially as they are embodied in the major constellations of images that serve as models for interpreting the world and for human behavior.

The image constellations live in interaction with human society. They are generally pluralistic, yet certain groups articulate more than peripheral images what is seen as the source of power and therefore the major touchstone of interpretation of the world so far as it is humanly significant. In primordial hunting society, evidenced by cave paintings and bear sacrifices, the animal in life and death is clearly the dominating image—giver of meat, tester of human strength, embodiment of mystery. It is manifest over and over that the hunter not only wants to challenge his prey, but also to "be" the bear or deer. After the agricultural revolution, the main images center around the plant, whose drama of life, death, and new life becomes the archetype of so much else. sacrifice, headhunting, initiation, the savior.

But around the fifth century B.C.E. the focus changed dramatically and, in historical terms, suddenly. This is the period called by the philosopher Karl Jaspers the "Axial Age."[1] We shall speak of it preeminently as the era of the Discovery of History and shall focus on the spiritual crisis it entailed and the resolution it produced in the form of the major religious founders and their Great Religions. For the Axial Age was an era of the emergence of great literate and historical cultures, empires, and world religions.

Elsewhere, Jaspers had written that there is a "sense of history only if events are understood as the objective premises of our present existence and at the same time as something else, something which has been—and in having been, was for itself—singular in time and unique in kind."[2] Behind the changes of the Axial Age, beyond doubt, lay a new awareness of time, or more precisely of a new kind of time. For one could only have the existential awareness of history requisite to establish spiritual (and cultural) forms to deal with it if one has grasped the one-way character of time: events have happened that are unique, have passed and will not come again, yet affect the present and indeed are its foundation.

The Great Religions that arose in this era were centered not on beast or grain, but on the sacred person—the prophet, the enlightened one or savior—and the sacred book. Both emerged in a moment of historical time deemed to have special, pivotal significance for all human experience. As Mircea Eliade has shown, for the "cosmic religion" of early hunters and agriculturalists, the *illud tempus*—the mythical time when the gods were supremely active and the ultimate meaning of the world was revealed—was the time of creation, typically reenacted at New Year's, with its ritual return to chaos and renewed order.

For the Great Religions, however, a moment *in* time, the time of the Buddha, the Christ, or the Prophet, becomes the moment of a second and even more powerful creation. In practical sacred importance, it exceeds the first creation; it is the centerpoint when "the hopes and fears of all the years are met" in a great new divine event associated with the work of an ideal, archetypal person, and with the generation of a sacred text bearing witness to it and the truths associated with it. Rather than the plant or animal, the master images of religion are now the person, the text, and the historical time in which divine purposes are worked out. Insofar as religion means images connecting inner and outer, we may think of the formation of the Great Religions as the emergence of a single image, or closely knit cluster of related images, at the center, with the repression of all others.

The image can be usefully understood in terms of the archetypal psychology of James Hillman and his premier interpreter, Roberts Avens.[3] For them, the image is that which dwells in the "imaginal realm," in the term of Henry Corbin, the distinguished scholar of Islamic mysticism. Imaginal reality is between the material on the one hand, and intellectual or spiritual (in the sense of ultimate reality) on the other. This realm must not be taken to have the negative connotations of "imagination" as the mere fanciful construction of ephemeral entities in the mind, for it discovers ways of knowing our pluralistic universe appropriate to our ultimate instrument of understanding, consciousness or psyche. The old gods may inhabit this terrain, but so also do the half-conscious images and mythologies that activate the rationalist and the atheist, the scientist and the logician, the sensualist no less than the ascetic. For do these not also enter their life roles in response to seeing a picture of an archetypal embodiment of the rationalist or scientist in the mind?

The imaginal realm is not imposed on the world; rather, it is one with our knowledge of the world; it is *how* we know, as we make what we know relevant to ourselves. The religious image then, again, is crucial to religion as a kind of language linking the three orders of image—nature, art, subjectivity. As Owen Barfield has vividly put it, it is erroneous to think of early man making myths and gods by "always projecting his insides onto something or other," as thought the world were dead till we gave it a fictive life. The truth is rather the reverse: "it was not man who made the myths but myths or the archetypal substance they reveal, which made man."[4] For man perhaps had no "insides" until myth and religion, working in profound exchange with the sense data of nature and the raw feelings, gave them to him.

The imaginal way of knowing is inherently polytheistic, and therefore so also is primordial human nature. For imaginalism handles in consciousness terms the "working" world of pluralistic reality. To it whatever ultimate unity there may be—whether represented by a king of the gods, Zeus or Amon, or a more abstract principle, Brahman or Ma'at—is in effect just another image associated with a particular state of awareness, that of mystical oneness with the All.

But the rise of the Great Religions meant, on the imaginal level, the establishment of a single image as sovereign and the subordination of all other images to it, or else their expulsion as demonic or nonexistent, gods of wood or stone. Yet the newly sovereign image is still a word from the primordial vocabulary. Again, Barfield has put it interestingly: "Every man, certainly every original man has something new to say, something new to mean. Yet if he wants to express that meaning . . . he must use language—a vehicle which presupposes that he must either mean what was meant before or talk nonsense."[5]

Certainly, if our talk is not nonsense, religion is a language par excellence, and never did it have anything more radically new to say than in the inception of the Great Religions, when heavensful of gods and spirits were brought under one true God, or one unified state of consciousness, like that of the Buddha under the tree of enlightenment, or the one Tao of which the Chinese sage spoke. Yet the language was still that of religion, for that was what such words had meant before. This meant that into the new unities came all the baggage of religion, not to be trashed but to be rearranged around a single center, to which all the rituals and myths and hierarchies would point. What would not fit in that pattern was, of course, discarded. But often it did not go quietly, leaving demoted gods and rites as the familiars or magic of popular religion, or more consequentially as voiceless yet lingering images in the psyche. For, no question about it, advancing only one image to the throne of heaven can be done only by main force, and there is bound to be wreckage, some of it strewn with shards and sharp splinters, and some of it not quite dead.

Yet the birth of the Great Religions was inevitable; one can hardly imagine it not happening in the course of human events. There was, of course, preparation. The background of the discovery of history was the growth of archaic agricultural states and especially the ancient riverine empires based on large-scale hydraulic works, though interestingly the great Founders tended to come not from these empires as such, but from smaller pastoral or farming territories on their fringes. For most of the ancient empires were mass peasant societies offering only marginal sustenance. Yet they afforded augmented division of labor, which led to some sense of unique individuality and role at least for an elite, and some surplus wealth that allowed for classes of religious and intellectual specialists—priests, contemplatives, and philosophers who could offer models of the ideal spiritual person and so advance the ideal of the spiritual person as an archetype, an image becoming more and more deeply embossed. For everyone, no doubt, the very existence of a complex society suggested the possibility of significant individual choices. The growth of technology increased trade and travel, with exposure to other cultures and ways of worship. So did wars of conquest, with the marching back and forth of armies and the taking of slaves. All in all, the ancient empires meant countless people uprooted from familiar village and shrine, thrown into burgeoning urban centers where they had neither roots nor familiar gods. In such a situation one is left to oneself to find images that work and experience that is convincing. Just before the dawn of the Great Religions we find the idea of individual salvation as a personal project rapidly growing in Egypt, Greece, and India.

Another important idea in the ancient empires was the sacred king, who would as in Babylon ritually fight the forces of chaos annually, or as in China plow the first furrow to begin the agricultural year. He too represented the life of humanity and the forces of the cosmos concentrated in one archetypal person. So, in another way, did the prophet, the voice of the gods in the world, and in the lineage of the archaic shaman. Significantly, Jesus, the supreme religious founder, is prophet, priest, and king in traditional Christian theology.

Despite the subterranean currents flowing in another direction, however, the age of the ancient empires was overtly the heyday of polytheism. The pantheons became more and more packed as the many peoples and tribes who conjoined to make up vast empires added their deities, and the bureaucracy of heaven expanded to match the increasing complexity of society below. Yet the contrivance of many polytheistic systems doubtless brought them subtly out of synchronization with the natural images of the psyche within. At least, no such overloaded pantheon could truly match the psyche of any particular individual. True, imperial polytheism, through its patronage of art and story, often enhanced the individuality of the gods. But that did not belie the deep-seated urge for some pivot, some sovereign center of meaning and supreme image, which would bring all things into order. But before that transition, with all its gain and loss, could happen, the ancient spiritual crisis had to be exacerbated by the discovery of history, which made the old chaos of gods seem not only confusing but menacing.

Its direct background, like that of the scriptural text that was to become so prominent a feature of the Great Religions, was the invention of writing. At first it may have been mostly of commercial use, but in time it recorded history and sacred words of power. Combined with ancient oral traditions of holy myth and mantic formulas, whose very sounds held transcendent energy, writing captured the words surrounding the pivotal moment of sacred history. To this day the most sacred power of the text, though written, is oral and auditory, the solemn reading of scripture in religious service, the chanting, recitation, or singing of Bible, Veda, or Koran. Yet the application of writing created the religious icon of the sacred text, a locus of the sacred that, though

perhaps dimly foreshadowed in the pictograph or the hiero-
glyphic charm, is essentially coeval with the Great Religions.

The discovery of history was a consequence of record keeping.
Though at first perhaps no more than a succession of kings and
victories, even the most primitive records would have engendered
a sense of things changing and not changing back. Recorded
events were always in danger of moving beyond mythical models
to become unique and irreversible events in *our* time, which must
be handled by us for our day. Even a chronicle of kings can tell us
that our kings are but epigoni of their great progenitors, but also
that those predecessors lived in a time within history like ours, not
in some mythical *illud tempus*.

Whether recorded or not, the disruption of local patterns by
empires like the Greek or Roman, or the time of the warring states
following on the decline of the Chou dynasty in China, could not
but bring home to ordinary people the vicissitudes of time as now
experienced and remembered. Human life, needless to say, has
always been uncertain, but now its disruptions came from peoples
much farther away than the next valley, people of queer tongue
and strange gods, who might carry off captives or demand the
community plant new crops and give the first fruits to an alien
lord. Such events would be unique, and unique events—whether
conquering armies, plague, or famine—were usually bad for ordinary people. With the discovery of history therefore came, on
many levels from dislocation in the realm of psychic images to
disasters with which one had to cope, what Eliade called the terror
of history, the fear of onrushing irreversible time full of uncer-
tainty and probable horror. It was this with which the custodians
of the sacred now had to contend.

The establishment religion of the ancient empires was essentially the province of the priestly/bureaucratic class responsible for
the state's orderly functioning: the scribes of Egypt, the *shih* of old
China. Honoring structure and continuity above all, it pleased
them to place above the personal gods an eternal regulative principle, Ma'at, Ŗta, or Tao, even as particular kings were but the
shadow of the principle of kingship. In their cosmogonies, creation and apocalypse were clearly less welcome than order; to
creation they significantly preferred in practice a primal meta-
historical era of model kings or sage emperors who represented
imperishable paradigms for the present. But now time, as change,

threatened to run out of control off the regulative tracks and destroy the timeless.

The discovery of history was thus a crucial challenge to religion, at least as crucial as that posed millennia earlier by the discovery of agriculture and the new orientation of humanity to the earth it wrought. Religion had, as always, pointed to realities transcendent over self and world, realities before which those entities could only be contingent, and time a matter of cosmic religion's "eternal return." Now religion must handle in some way the reality of irreversible time and its correlate, the possibility that humans can make individual, irreversible choices within it or, conversely, suffer its unpredictable terrors involuntarily.

Like the earlier challenge, historical time was profoundly unwelcome to religion, threatening its most fundamental structures and seeming to open the door to its oldest and greatest enemy, cosmic chaos. It implied a world wherein no law or god was in charge, and anything, however bad, could happen without reason or regard to moral deserts. Indeed, so awesome was the terror of historical time that most ancients could not, or did not, face it full and put in place a counterfoil to its horror without entirely realizing what the enemy was. Nonetheless, an examination of important features of religion in the Discovery of History era, the Axial Age, suggests the nature of the age's deep-seated spiritual crisis. Responses to history follow four main strands, sometimes separate alternatives and sometimes intertwined: epic, ritual, the religious founders, and wisdom.

Epic

One response is to accept history but to see it as the unfolding of divine purpose—the triumph of a particular people or dynasty, the defeat of the powers of darkness by God. Thus history, with its wars and tribulations, is granted reality, but its terror is defanged by transcendent purpose. Much of the great narrative literature of the era of the Discovery of History has this basic motif: the historical and prophetic books of the Hebrew Scriptures, the Kojiki in Japan, the Aeneid.

Ritual

Another response is to keep certain rites, such as those of a court, a city, or an official priesthood and its shrines, unchanged as a sort of frozen perpetuation of the past before the discovery of history. Thus representing one area of experience untouched by the ambiguities of historical time, timeless ritual becomes a counterweight to history. In ancient Rome, the institution of the vestal virgins and the sacrifices of the city's official priesthood remained virtually unchanged through all the historical vicissitudes of the empire until the triumph of Christianity. In ancient Japan, an imperial princess was sent far away from the court to the Saigū, or abstinence palace, near the Grand Shrine of Ise, the Shinto shrine of the imperial ancestral deities. There she avoided all Buddhist practice and even words. She thus represented in her Shinto purity and ritual acts the court not as it was, but as it would like to be seen by the primordial gods.

The Religious Founders

The most consequential response to the Discovery of History, however, and the most momentous religious event of the millennium beginning around the fifth century B.C.E., was the life and work of the great religious founders. Only a half dozen or so persons have filled this awesome vocation, becoming the pivotal figures of religions embracing hundreds of millions of persons, washing over vast geographical areas, and lasting fifteen to twenty-five centuries. They are Zoroaster, the Buddha, Confucius, Lao-tze, Jesus, and Muhammad. (Others, especially the Hebrew lawgivers and prophets, and the Vedantic sages of India, have had a comparable role within their traditions.) Although their stories are encrusted with myth and legend, with the possible exception of Lao-tze they were undoubtedly real persons, and all incarnate the way in which the person—though he may point beyond himself—has become the central focus of the new religious style. Three of them—the Buddha, Jesus, and Muhammad—knowingly or not, went an important step beyond the others by founding the world's three major missionary and transcultural religions, faiths that went far outside the boundaries of their homelands to draw the bulk of their adherents from distant places and to become the foundational religion of many otherwise diverse cultures.

In all cases, the founder represents a fresh response to history. The other responses are little more than a special case of characteristics of primordial religion, but the major religious founder is a new development, and so far as we know, one unique to his millennium, unknown before and since. At the dawn of history as we know it, he represents a person who, while living in a discrete, identifiable moment of historical time, exemplifies or communicates a reality far greater than it, to which historical time is subject. The message is encapsulated in scripture and perpetuated through sacred gestures, acts, and institutions: sacraments, forms of prayer, ethical values; sangha, church, ulama, mandarins.

By making the life of a single individual the pivot of history, the founder religions acknowledge history's irreversible movement and at the same time give it a sharply focused central axis. By emphasizing the drama of a single and unique life as the bearer of revelation, they show that now, in the more complex, diversified, and uncertain life of a "modern" society, the significant individual—and not just tribal custom—is what counts. This is reflected all the more in the fact that these religions, although much fortified by institutionalization, have in one way or another given recognition to the importance of individual response to their claims. This is displayed in the prominence they give such themes as karma or judgment: each individual will be held individually accountable for his or her faith and life, and will receive individually appropriate reward or retribution. In earlier religion, such individual reckoning was usually far hazier, more likely a tribal than a truly personal matter. But with the advent of the saving person as the central religious symbol comes the corresponding reality of the individually accountable person responding to it. We will return later to the theme of the religious founder.

Wisdom

Another way of transcending the onslaughts of historical time is through absolutizing states of consciousness or philosophical realizations in which the timeless manifests its incomparable superiority over temporality and history. Thus, mysticism and mystical metaphysics, emphasizing the oneness of all things with the Absolute and the illusory nature of conditioned reality, were potent forces in the period of the Discovery of History. In India, at approximately the same time as the emergence of the founders, sages in the tradition that was to become Hinduism produced such works as the Upanishads and the Bhagavad-Gita. In them the central theme is the inner unity of the individual self, who seems to suffer the vicissitudes of time and history, with the supreme Self, who changes not. In the West, philosophers such as those of the Platonic and Neoplatonic movements offered broadly comparable visions, declaring that inwardly blending the self with the One like two rings conjoining was better than clamoring after the empty glories of empires rising and falling with the tides of history. In time their contemplative vision was itself to be joined with the historical stream of Judaism and the Western founder religions, Christianity and Islam.

For in the founder faiths, a reaction in favor of mysticism and wisdom tended to set in, as we shall see, after the founder's day. The wise came to urge a perspective that stressed the timeless, divine essence behind the temporal career of the historical founder. Thus, in Buddhism, the Mahayana movement tended to downplay the historical Buddha in favor of realizing one's own buddhahood through oneness with the eternal Dharmakaya, the universal essence. Christianity, especially in the Greek theologians and mystics, and Islam also, moved through a "wisdom" stage in which the deepest emphasis was on grasping with mystically illumined insight the eternal reality of God that underlay the particulars of the revelation through Jesus or Muhammad.

Yet the founder religions and what they implied about the human carried the day. The other responses to the crisis of the Discovery of History, in the end, were largely incorporated into them or their Judaic and Hindu equivalents. The founder religions made use of epic, especially as prolegomena showing how God or destiny prepared for the supreme revelation in the sacred person, as in Christian use of the Hebrew Scriptures or the Buddhist popularity of the Jataka tales, stories of the founder's previous lives. The founder religions generously employed ritual,

"Jesus Christ Raises Lazarus." Reprinted from Johann Friedrich Overbeck, *The Holy Gospels* (New York: Appleton, 1856), illus. 40.

with its sacred time and space, to perpetuate the memory of the founder, and indeed to recreate spiritually the time when his holy feet walked the earth. As we have seen, these faiths also acquired mystical dimensions.

But the ruling image was the founder, the transcendent with a human face. Millennia after the obscurity of the few human beings who shared the cave paintings with magnificent animals, and the potent yet stereotyped roles of shamans and sacred kings, emerged sacred revelation in the form of a person of distinctive character and appeal, capable of saying or doing unexpected things that nonetheless made surprising sense when all put together.

The rare founder vocation, then, calls for an especially comprehensive religious personality. The founder must himself be an image that mirrors, and brings together in a convincing new pattern, the diverse spiritual needs and aspirations of his day. Characteristically he appears at a time when important changes are afoot in his society, through powerful intercultural contact like that of Aryan and Dravidian in the Buddha's day, or the Hellenistic mix in Jesus', or through dynastic decline and civil war, as in Confucius's and Lao-tze's. The old order is seen by many to be outmoded; events have shattered its framework and splintered its light. In times like these, religious language and symbol are still effective, but a half-conscious awareness has come that it must be shaped into new configurations, illumined from a fresh angle and reinforced by a powerful new symbol of legitimacy and authority, to work today.

At the same time, the new religion must maintain enough symbols of continuity with the old, established religion to be able to draw on its legitimacy, as did Christianity with Judaism or Confucianism with the old "Sinism" of the *Book of Rites*. It must not offend the many for whom too sharp a break with the spiritual past, at least on the level of symbol and practice, would be highly disconcerting. Rather, the new founder faith does best when it can show that the new does not reject, but instead fulfills, the old, bringing out its plenary but thus far unspoken potential, so that people can say, "This was really true all the time, but we didn't realize it till now." The Buddha, therefore, did not directly attack the brahmins or the Vedas, but instead implied that what he taught merely perfected what was already a tendency within Hinduism, to emphasize inner enlightenment rather than priesthood or rite.

The effective founder, then, must follow a very delicate tack, one neither too radical nor too conservative, revealing something significant that is new while maintaining a sense of meaningful continuity with what went before. Like Jesus, he must fulfill rather than destroy the Law and the Prophets; like the Buddha, teach his listeners to be lamps unto themselves, finding their own salvation through meditation and the unblinking analysis of the Four Noble Truths, while exercising discretion in his relations with authority and following the familiar ancient way of the wandering ascetic and sage.

Likewise, the founder must be spiritually accessible to a wide spectrum of the people. Again like Jesus and the Buddha, he must be able to appeal to the poor and voice some of their concerns, while also winning friends and supporters among the elite, even among the established priestly class. He must have a message both for the general public and for a loyal, closely knit band of disciples who will be a nucleus of the institutionalization of his work. He must have something for those of activist and contemplative temper. He must appeal to both men and women.

All these imposing qualities were necessary for the founders of the Axial Age in their great task of transforming religion from its archaic cosmic, communal nature to the Great Religions of history. At the same time, we must recognize that the founder does not so much radically innovate as redirect and revalorize religious motifs already present. He himself is but a "super" version of the immemorial shaman and priest; his scriptures are but a written extension of archaic myth, chronicle, chant, and god-possessed mutterings. Indeed, at least some of his scriptures, like the Confucian classics and the Hebrew Bible known to Jesus, already may have been written and canonized. Few specific symbols and practices of the Great Religions are wholly new to them. Like the cosmic religion themes of Christmas, they simply take on new meanings and slightly new configurations while maintaining the overtones of the old.

Nonetheless, the Great Religions make a new departure. Besides centering in a new way on the individual person, both of the founder and of those who individually turn to him as the focus of spiritual power and revelation, they embody a constellation of distinctively presented, if not entirely novel, features that will cast a long ray of light down the religious future. These are (1) a sacred moment in historical time; (2) a single central personal symbol; (3) a definite canon of scripture; (4) a definite process of salvation; and (5) definite models of human nature and ultimate reality.

A Sacred Moment in Historical Time

As we have seen, for the cosmic type of religion, whether the old Babylonian and Egyptian or Shinto today, the major festival is New Year's. Its celebration suggests a symbolic return to primordial chaos and a recapitulation of creation, the ritual defeat of the monster of chaos by the hero or the lighting of a new fire. But the Great Religions, while acknowledging the first creation, make central the second, the time of the founder and the saving events associated with him. Distinctive events in historical time define these religions' experience and mark their sacred calendars: Passover, Wesek commemorating the Buddha's birth and enlightenment, Christmas and Easter, the Islamic month of the hajj. The events behind them are akin to the creation of a world, and in a sense are even greater than that primal act, for they are both the culmination of the creation and the rectification of what went wrong with it.

A Single Central Personal Symbol

We have already discussed the transformative significance of the emergence of the archetypal person as the supreme medium of revelation, of making the universe humanly meaningful, in the Great Religions. We must emphasize also that even the appearance of gods as beings full of "human" personality and capable of emotional interaction with humans, as in Hindu bhakti or the variegated Taoist pantheon, rather than one-dimensional archetypes or centers of sheer numinosity, was broadly speaking a product of the same Axial Age that produced the founders, or even a consequence of it.

A Definite Canon of Scripture

Precursors of the role of scripture in the Great Religions of course exist, such as the Pyramid Texts of Egypt and the orally transmitted Vedas of India. But the place of texts in the Great Religions is special. They are not timeless power formulas or myths, but words coming directly out of the sacred event, whether narratives leading up to or embracing it, or the discourse of the founder himself, or letters and tracts of his close disciples. Characteristically, in the Great Religions the canon of scripture is more sharply defined than in even those archaic faiths that were literate; in the former, one knows precisely which texts are "in" and which "out."

This definiteness is of a piece with the Great Religions' drive toward a high level of self-definition in many areas. They want to make clear who is a member of each and who is not, who is saved and who is not, what is true and what is heresy, where the boundaries are on all dimensional planes. Scripture confirms that the right doctrines, practices, and institutions are not merely subjective or ambiguous realities, but can be demarcated publicly and verbally. Further, it shows they are clearly connected to historical events—the same events that produced the founder and the subsequent canon—and define one's role as a physical or spiritual soldier in the armies of light.

Although views regarding the exact nature of scriptural authority vary both within and between Great Religions, all believers would grant that their sacred texts possess a unique authority setting them apart from all other books, and requiring that their words be received with special reverence. As both parent and child of such a unique book, the authority of the Great Religion itself is ratified. Indeed, the whole issue of authority in religion is raised to a new pitch as the authority of priesthoods (or ministeriums) and scriptures intermix, and the assertion of objective truth in religion rises to high prominence with the highly rigorous self-definition of the Great Religions.

Definite Process of Salvation

Similar to the enhancement of scriptural authority in the Great Religions is the process of the definition of teaching concerning salvation. First we must note that, unlike much tribal and archaic religion, the Great Religions tend to emphasize individual salvation in this life and the life to come. To be sure, a growing trend in this direction in archaic religion—whether in the soteriology of the Hellenistic mystery religions or the growing stress on karma and reincarnation in India—is part of the background of the great faiths. The Axial Age, with its crisis of emergent individual awareness, posed the question before submitting the final answers.

But as in the case of the terror of history, the full dimensions of the abyss of radical individualism opens up, with its potential for ultimate choice and ultimate aloneness, only to transcend it in the same thought: in heaven, in nirvana, in the Tao, in the Confucian good society. The Great Religions have thus centered on single simple sure keys to salvation out of the terrors of history and individualism: faith in Christ, love of God, submission to God's will, meditation. Techniques have varied within religions themselves, involving controversy and different practice on the role of sacraments, bhakti devotionalism, or lay and monastic versions of Buddhism. But the individual believer is usually presented with a clear path to salvation, if he or she chooses to follow it, by priests and preachers.

Definite Models of Human Nature and Ultimate Reality

The path to salvation of the Great Religions applies an equally definite model to human and divine nature, though its doctrinal articulation may undergo development. A fundamental model or root metaphor will appear: the human being as child of God, a wave on the sea of infinite reality, the product of karma. God will be seen in corresponding terms, as personal deity, as impersonal Absolute, as the negation of all conditioned reality.

These concepts, like the others, help define the religion and set it over against others, for obviously only one teaching on such final and urgent issues can be correct; those who believe wrongly about God himself do so at their own peril. At the same time, religious beliefs concerning human nature have a powerful— though frequently convoluted rather than straightforward—interaction with the cultures in which they dwell. Art and literature may reflect some aspects of the spiritual view of human nature, engaging with such themes as the moral responsibility of the child of God, or the plasticity of the expression of divine infinity; but they will characteristically explore it to its ultimate limits and even react against it while not able quite to free themselves from the fundamental image.

The emergence of the Great Religions entailed spiritual loss as well as gain. Cosmic religion possessed an equilibrium and nuanced sense of the sacred scattered through the universe at an opposite pole from the Great Religions' tendency to focus around single events, symbols, centers of value. The old polytheism was a matter of quality as well as quantity, seeing the divine in a different way from monotheism. It perceived discrete gods in a diversity of places, moods, and persons; in violent and calm, new and old, male and female. Inevitably, something of this quality crept back into the Great Religions in the culti of saints, angels; and heavenly pantheons, yet even those benign principalities and powers were subservient to a single Lord or spiritual path, servants of one who, like the Buddha, was "teacher of gods and men." The Great Religions sacrificed equilibrium for purpose, and rather than answering to all needs or fulfilling all potential symbols chose those that fit the historical destiny each saw for itself.

A good example is the relative role of male and female. Despite later pious claims to the contrary, in virtually every instance the rise of the Great Religions meant a marked lessening of feminine presence in spiritual life, both on the symbolic and practical levels.[6] Goddesses, priestesses, and shamanesses alike were displaced by a new faith whose founder was inevitably male, and whose disciples and successors in the leadership of the movement were also male, and whose scriptures were written by males.

The social order envisioned by the new faith was also thoroughly patriarchal. In this respect it did not, to be sure, usually differ from its predecessor, but the male-dominated order here below was now reinforced by a male deity or equivalent above, whose chief earthly representatives were likewise male. Thus in China the rise of the Confucian order was marked by decrees against the practices of female shamanesses and "witches"; in the

West the rise of the great monotheistic faiths militated against the cults of Isis and Ishtar. Monasticism, a prominent feature of several of the Great Religions, was likewise antifeminine insofar as it implied the potential completeness of male spirituality and spiritual authority without significant contact with the feminine. The ideal held up even to nuns was usually the overcoming of all that was female and physical in order to approximate, at least, the spiritual male.

Another loss was the sense of reciprocity between religions that characterized cosmic and archaic religion. Although one divine patron might send his clan into war against another, there was a sense in which it was recognized that all gods were more or less the same. One worshiped the gods of wherever one went, and some went so far as to see, as Apuleius did of the Great Mother, that they were one going under many names: Isis, Ishtar, Cybele, or Aphrodite. But, as we have seen, the Great Religions brought a greater exclusiveness. Faiths were decisively right or wrong. That realization could, of course, be taken as advance insofar as it represented a heightened respect for consistency. As such it doubtless went with the heightened meaning of free, separate individual existence. One defines oneself, at least in part, through consistent behavior and regard for objective truth. Yet some might feel the older religions better appreciated the limits of logical rigor in exploring the world of the spirit.

To balance off the losses, however, was a great new reality. Religion was now set on a relatively fast and irreversible course of historical development. Each Great Religion began with an implicit program, a history ready to unfold expeditiously. The plus was that the religion then had some capacity both to vigorously make history and to adjust to changing historical circumstances; the danger was that its program might be exhausted, its coinage all spent, well before the end of world history. But for better or worse, embedded in each Great Religion was the presupposition that, in the postmodernist phrase, a "Grand Narrative" was to be narrated as the religion actively took on its task of doing the will of God, converting the world and building the ideal society.

We need finally to talk about religious change. How did the great change of the Axial Age transpire, and how the subsequent transitions we shall describe?

Religious change is governed by two basic forces, pressure

internal to the religion and pressure external to it. Needless to say, these two are in complex interaction as Berger's projection, reification, and internalization chain creates external conditions out of internal, and vice versa. Yet, historically as well as individually, the two need to be separated. We need to try to discern when, or in what ways, a religion is changing because of needs inherent in its own structure and history, and when it is responding to forces in its environment. Admittedly, the issue will rarely be simple in practice. Religions may be forced to respond to outside circumstances they themselves had a hand in creating, and a changing world may affect deep subjective feelings the experiencer believes are purely religious. Yet, on both individual and historical levels, the effort needs to be made to sort out the internal and external pressures. Religions have their own internal developmental agendas based on a working out of the program implicit to their basic vision, and they also respond to changes in the world around them.

The social scientific study of religion has tended to emphasize the role of the external force. For example, in the study of new religious movements, a long tradition assigns their origin to intercultural tensions and conditions of repression or "relative deprivation." As far back as 1913 Alexander F. Chamberlain wrote of "new religions" occurring as a product of the meeting of native and "higher" peoples. The new faiths, he said, make use of incompletely understood ideas brought by traders, settlers, missionaries, and colonial officials.[7]

In 1943 Ralph Linton wrote of "nativist movements." In contrast to the attempted assimilation of Chamberlain's "new religions," these are "any conscious, organized attempt on the part of a society's members to revive or perpetuate selected aspects of its culture" when the society is undergoing rapid change; as in the Native American Ghost Dance, the perpetuated cultural features are given highly symbolic if not magical value.[8] Anthony F. C. Wallace described what he called a "revitalization movement" typically started by a charismatic prophet to construct "a more satisfying culture" in times of cultural disorientation.[9] In the same way, Neil J. Smelser's "value-oriented movement" arises in times of ferment and stress, and when alternative—that is, nonreligious— means for reconstituting the social situation are perceived as unavailable.[10] These perceptions of new religious movements, like many others that could be cited, presuppose a "crisis-response" view of their generation, and more broadly a view of religion as a passive but fluid entity only responding to external pressures.

This understanding, however, leaves some unanswered questions regarding new religious movements and religion as a whole. First, it does not explain why some crises of stress, rapid social change, and apparent discrediting of old values produce new religious movements, and others do not. Japan's devastation and defeat in World War II, for example, is widely held to have set the stage for the postwar exfoliation there of new religions, yet no comparable phenomenon took place in her erstwhile allies, Germany and Italy.

On the other hand, some new religions appear to arise spontaneously or out of opportunity, rather than from any discernible crisis much beyond the normal anxiety of human affairs. One thinks of the rise of spiritualism, adventism, and communal movements in the young American republic of the 1840s, or the growth of new religious movements in the "youth culture" of the 1960s, which—despite tension over Vietnam and civil rights—was not a time of trauma comparable to that suffered by colonialized peoples or Japan in 1945.

Several critics have pointed out that crisis-response models such as those cited above fail adequately to take into account that religious movements are, after all, *religious*. Bryan Wilson writes that although the preservation of a threatened culture, or the creation of a new society, may be implicit in a religious movement, it is not usually the group's own main intention or principal feature. In the religionist's own mind the *religious* objectives of giving salvation, magical power, or heightened mystical experience have preeminence.[11]

H. Byron Earhart, writing on the new religions of Japan, argues that a religious tradition has longstanding needs and drives of its own that cannot be overlooked in understanding why a movement derivative from it has arisen or taken the form that it has.[12] We would agree, noting that this is particularly the case with the long histories of the Great Religions. Their origins, while in a sense certainly expressing potential latent in religion from the human beginning, may rightly be understood historically as response to the crisis engendered by the discovery of history and all the secular factors that went into the enhancement of individualism—though noting with Wilson that their own conscious intention put it in the form of salvation and sacred experience. But the religions' subsequent history is surely as much an exploration of potential forms of expression implicit in the faith from its inception as it is a response to external vicissitudes. The real pressure is very often from within, as in a balloon being inflated; the outer circumstances may shape the form it takes, particularly by setting limits to what is culturally acceptable.

Buddhism, for instance, began as a religion whose central practice was the concentration or meditation that stops the suffering-desire syndrome. Implicit, therefore, was the question: what is meditation? Is any practice that stops mental action, and so frees one from the mental roots of suffering and desire, meditation in the Buddhist sense? The historical answer came as Buddhism explored several "at the limits" possibilities: the quasi-magical rituals of Vajrayana, the simple act of faith of Pure Land, Nichiren chanting.

Religions explore possibilities such as these not only because various interpretive options may be more or less congruent with the various cultures into which the faith moves, but also because individuals attracted to the faith are eager to know what it can do. They want to discover what new kinds of experience it can offer and what classes of surety it provides. Hōnen, the Japanese father of Pure Land Buddhism, said that he had read the Buddhist canon of scripture five times, but found no peace till, through faith in Amida Buddha's vow to save all who called upon his name, he depended on *tariki,* the power of another, rather than *jiriki,* one's own power. It was, to be sure, a time of strife and change in medieval Japan. Yet for this quiet, reclusive monk the battle was inward and involved a search toward the far limits of Buddhist meaning. For him *tariki,* though not meditation in any customary sense, most adequately fulfilled its promise for him because it expressed, through depending on another rather than on oneself for salvation, the ultimate meaning of the Buddhist negation of ego. Salvation through faith was therefore truly at the heart of Buddhism, though it took the religion many centuries fully to realize this.

Religious change basically is induced when subjective experience is found dissonant with the religion's practical reification. Hōnen, like Luther, came to experience his religion's ritual and institutionalization to be at odds with what he inwardly knew the same religion to mean. As we have seen, religion is fundamentally the story of images linking the subjective world with the social reification of the same, in rites and public ideas and institutions dealing with the transcendent and the human place in the cosmos. But what happens when distance appears between inner and outer, whether because of social change or the individual's own need to explore?

Change must then take place to get them together. The person may first try to change subjectively. But if this does not work and pressure does not relent, he or she will be driven to change the outer instead, shaping it to fit the subjective model. Often the extent of change can be minimized and many innocuous symbols of continuity maintained; at other times major rearrangements are called for, since it has become important not only to tinker with the outer expressions of reality but also, in the process, to adopt a new flag—to symbolically stress invigorating change rather than reassuring continuity. Either way, change takes place and change makes history.

The Great Religions are *religions with a history*. They have a history not only from the point of view of the outside observer—from which all religion, however "cosmic," has a history inasmuch as things have happened in it over time—but the idea of history is inherent in their own inner experience. Their scriptures, shrines, chronicles, churches, and temples all posit as their reason for being events that happened in real historical time. Perhaps some of those histories are mythical, but they are nonetheless significant for the view of time they assume. The Christian cult of the saints, which replaced the polytheistic gods and goddesses of archaic Mediterranean religion, differed from what went before in several important respects. The saints represented the sacred in human flesh, not divine nature, and moreover in the flesh of persons who had acted significantly at specific times and places in human history—as martyrs, apostles, bishops.[13]

For it must be realized that history is not a given, nor a work of nature unaided. It is a human phenomenon, a product of human consciousness both as process and as awareness of that process. Just as history as we know it unveils the expanding scope of human awareness and ability as we move from one tier of civilization to another, so thinking of the process *as history*—as irreversible and accelerating change—is a way of thinking associated with one stage of that process. There is a history of history. Like religion, it is an image relating the human to the ultimate, grounded in subjectivity and projected on the world as it interprets the world.

Marxism may be the last and most rigorous attempt to reify the history image as objectively true in the outer world as it is in its inner sources and in reflection. But the Great Religions have gone in the same direction, perceiving irreversible divine purpose in the drift of events. We have noted how deconstructionism and postmodernism have endeavored to counter that perception, arguing in effect that in fact the universe, including the human universe, is naught but radical pluralism. It is a diverse collection of happenings and human experiences with no more than free-associational links one to another. But by believing in their own histories the Great Religions have made history, both as fact and concept.

It is interesting to compare the Great Religions' unitary view of history, and of ultimate reality, with the pluralism of such post-Jungians as James Hillman and Robert Avens, whom we have already mentioned, and who are clearly linked to postmodernism. Here human consciousness is a labyrinthine cavern of images with neither beginning nor end, though the light may shift from one to another. For the post-Jungians, as therapists of the soul, the great human temptation is to see, or rather force, unity (monism) that subordinates one entity for the sake of another, instead of seeing and living each image just as it is. James Hillman has argued against the constricting role of the idea of an ego, which he identifies with the hero figure, conquering and overcoming. As heroes we "ascend" at the cost of not fulfilling potential for multiplicity and diversity, and ultimately our conquest is futile, as the human ego, however heroic, in the end goes down to Sheol. Wholeness, for Hillman, is not this sort of sterile ego integrity, but is a self at home with a multiplicity of imaginal presentations, each received with joy in its own time. It envisions a human life as the embodiment of a sequence of many gods. Hillman declares, "Polytheistic psychology would not suspend the commandment to have 'no other gods before me,' but would extend that commandment for each mode of consciousness."[14]

Understandably, Hillman is skeptical of ideas of "spiritual

growth" as a project of the imperial ego, as he is of the notion that
we ought to keep "growing" till we are in the grave. This is merely
a fixation on the maturation process of childhood and youth.
Adult life is not progressing "to" anything; it is rather, ideally, the
subtly and infinitely varied rounds of experience afforded by
fulfilled relationships and fertility on both the psychic and biological planes.

In this light, the Great Religions are adolescent religions. Indeed, that image illumines much about them: their thirst for truth
and commitment, their need to organize the world, their preoc-
cupation with the ego-self and its problematic, their view of historical and personal time as an arena for "growth" and the attain-
ment of success up to the ultimate conquest of all rivals. The Great
Religions, like "moderns" of all stamps, want to perceive in history,
especially religious history, a unity of direction in what may really
be an infinite array of image events in jumbled relation to one
another. Such events are not exactly random, yet neither do they
move in anything so simple as "straight-line" cause and effect.

Careful history itself brings this out. "Grand Narrative" styles of
historical writing, like that of Gibbon, have assumed that the
Christian cult of saints was a replacement for the old polytheism.
Detail work shows that, as we have seen, it was not the same in
important respects; although the assertion may contain broad
truth, saint honor developed differently in different places and
was consciously more closely related to Roman concepts of friend-
ship and patronage than polytheism.[15] It was an animation of new
ranges of faces in the cavern of images as much as the replacement of old with new in the same ranks.

The unity of history is itself an image, as real as any other in the
imaginal world between spirit and flesh. But like all images *in*
human history, and like most in individual human life, it has its
mysterious rise, its development by association with other images,
and its decay. The final stage would be that represented by the
final collapse of a religion into remnants, isolated myths, and folk
practice—the breakdown of an image of a unified cause into
separate images as the unity image is no longer sustainable, presumably because it is no longer the focal symbol of a unified,
heroic ego in a sufficient number of believers. (In the same way,
certain images in one's personal life—about oneself, one's rela-

tionships, one's beliefs—may fragment as disconfirmations accumulate and alternative images arise.)

Great Religions sink down to Sheol because of such an exhaustion of their original unifying language. They are ordinarily unable to accept nonunifying language by permitting themselves in polytheistic manner to be only one image of the sacred among many, since their original and ruling rationale was to unify subjective and outer images in one master image, one sovereign God, savior of all, or "teacher of gods and men." As we shall see, the last stage of a Great Religion, however, is as folk religion when, though unacknowledged, the master image has fragmented and the bonds linking religious imagery and the major institutions of society have also frayed or snapped.

Just because the Great Religions have a sense of history, of revelation and mission in history, they are open as well as closed to historical change. A conservative mandate, desiring only to maintain faith with the original revelation, can be found in all and is expressed by factions often labeled traditionalist or fundamentalist. But that must coexist with another notion inspired by the original opening: that new revelation *can* come in historical time, at the right *kairos*. A sense that religion can and must adapt to changing conditions while remaining true to its sources goes with acceptance of history, and must therefore consort with the limiting principle that only a certain amount of protean flexibility is latent in that fidelity. This is the source of endless conflict, and no one will know until a faith's last drop of life has drained into the sands of time what its full potential was. But since it stemmed from a single historical moment and a single definitive revelation, presumably there was some limit to how far the religion could adapt and still be itself in any meaningful way. Do all religions reach a point where they can adapt no more?

Before dealing with this question, we must turn to the story of the Great Religions themselves and their historical vicissitudes.

Chapter 4

The Development of the Great Religions

Our study of the history of the Great Religions will be based on a model that proposes they develop through five stages over a historical trajectory of some 2,500 years, though the length of each stage may vary considerably. These stages are: (1) apostolic, (2) wisdom and imperial, (3) devotional, (4) reformation, and (5) folk religion. Progress through these stages, as we have suggested, although obviously affected deeply by external conditions, is not wholly governed by response to them, but also follows an internal logic of religious history. They are, in our view, the natural succession of ways a religion, fundamentally a response to the Discovery of History crisis, develops the potential for expression latent in itself. All the stages refer back in some way to the problem of historical time, but also deal with a dissonance left unresolved by the preceding stage, or a sense that the earlier stage's potential has been exhausted.

At the same time, all these religions carried over a great deal of sacred baggage from previous religious eras, going back to the Paleolithic. They *are* religions, and emerged in a time when religious ways of thinking and symbol making were not widely questioned. The "dialectic of the sacred," the impingement of the supernatural on human life, the efficacy of rite, the power of holy scripture, and the necessity of state religion—all were powerful in the affairs of king and peasant alike in the Discovery of History era. The new Great Religions easily slipped into these traditional

68

forms of expression, though with new messages and new particulars, while providing foci around which all manner of things new and old, from sacred wells to metaphysical models, could be consolidated. As they accomplished this task, they permeated their environing society, then inevitably generated a new kind of society and a fresh cultural wave that changed the old and went on to bring vast new populations into history.

The supreme examples of this kind of religion are the three great truly international and cross-cultural faiths, all also founder religions: Buddhism, Christianity, and Islam. In addition, the traditional Chinese religious system, with Confucianism as its elite expression and its further mix of Taoism, Buddhism, ancestrism, and local culti, also has founders and in large part shares the same paradigm—so vast is China as to be itself almost a world, its ways have been a regional as well as a national foundation for life.

Historical Hinduism must also be considered a Great Religion for our purposes, though unlike the others it has no historical founder and therefore it is impossible to pinpoint a moment of origin. For our purposes, it is best to regard it as having started as a Great Religion, comparable to the others, around the first century C.E., at about the same time as Christianity. This was the era of the texts that have set the tone of all later Hinduism: the later Upanishads, the Bhagavad-Gita, the Laws of Manu, the Yoga Sutras. To them the earlier Vedas are a sort of Old Testament. This was the high point of Buddhism in India, against which Hinduism as a religion had to define itself, and it marks the early roots of bhakti and the lore of the great salvationist gods—Vishnu, Krishna, Shiva—who were to color medieval and modern devotional Hinduism so deeply.

On the other hand, no attempt will be made to fit Zoroastrianism, Judaism, and Shinto into the model. The evolution of Zoroastrianism does agree with the pattern for its first thousand years, but its career as a Great Religion was then abruptly cut short by the triumph of Islam in its Persian homeland. Judaism and Shinto (and also the smaller Indian religions, Jainism and Sikhism), not having become the long-term predominant religion of large culture areas, have had a very different sort of history. Surviving tribal religions also do not fit in, of course. But at least 90 percent of the human race now has, at least as the religion associated with their traditional culture, one of the five for whose destiny this model will be proposed—Buddhism, Chinese religion, Hinduism, Christianity, and Islam.

Though they all came out of the problems and prospects of the Axial Age, thereby reflecting a unique era whose like had never come before nor will come again, the five faiths did not arise simultaneously. Buddhism and the Chinese tradition are 500 years older than Christianity and Hinduism; Islam is 500 years younger. The development of the five has therefore been staggered in relation to one another. They are not all at the same stage of internal evolution, one factor that has not always been taken sufficiently into account by promoters of interreligious dialogue.

If our hypothesis is correct, then in the twentieth and twenty-first centuries we are seeing the effective demise of Buddhism and Chinese religion as major world religions; Christianity and Hinduism are entering their folk religion stage, surviving as popular faiths without a corresponding living Great Tradition; and Islam is just entering the reformation stage, corresponding to the Christianity of the age of Luther, Calvin, and Loyola. Much of the contemporary religious scene does indeed seem to bear out these bold-sounding assertions. We shall return later to a reading of the current religious situation.

As we have indicated, our perspective requires that we take very seriously the self-propelling internal dynamics of a religion, even of a religion lasting as long as twenty-five centuries. We have dealt with the issue of external versus internal stimuli of religious change. In thinking of stages of development of a Great Religion, we need to give due attention to the fact that a religion's response to environing conditions may be different at different times because of internal dynamics in the religion's own history. The extent of a religion's previous history, for example, conditions its self-image and therefore its appreciation of what its options are.

The immediate stimulus for religious change, then, may be external. It is likely to be something in a society's outer world that first suggests the dissonance between inner and outer that requires rectification. But the *way* in which the religion responds will surely be shaped by where it is in its own history. A religion has an internal need to do several things: to explore its full philosophical potential, to engender and interpret mystical experience, to connect with as much as possible of the human emotional range, to inspire art and rite, to offer homely symbols of its power to those in the humbler walks of life, and finally, when all this becomes too weighty, to find a capacity to reform and simplify itself. These are not needs imposed by external conditions; they are an internal agenda set by the mere fact that the movement is a religion, and it is in the nature of a religion to want to engage such areas of human experience as these. All have in common that they touch, or are believed to touch, the frontier between the human and the Transcendent, building symbol-laden bridges between the two; no religion worthy of the name could overlook establishing numerous bridgeheads along that boundary, though it may not be able to erect them all at once.

The particular historical stage will determine whether the response to an outer need for change is, say, an increase of its emotional spectrum through devotionalism or the self-simplification of reformation, or finally withdrawal to the folk religion level, when all the major creative responses inherent in the faith's original charter seem played out.

When a religion is in some alignment with the other major institutions of society, as it was in the medieval situation around the world, its challenge is to complement external hegemony with control of the entire subjective empire. Hence it advances the wide emotional range of devotionalism—Bernardine and Franciscan piety in Europe, bhakti in India, Sufism in Islam, Vajrayana and Pure Land Buddhism farther East.

When, as the world turns, rapport with the other institutions— political, economic, educational—begins to slip from religion's hands, first only in subtle yet felt ways, the response will be for reformation that seeks simplification, both to redress the overextended complexity of the devotional expression and to give it greater adaptability over against the world. Through reformation faith wants to recover full power in at least part of its world. This was the task of the Protestant Reformation in sixteenth-century Europe, Kamakura Buddhism in Japan, and the current Islamic revolution. It is a complex process of seeking to reestablish the religion's hegemony in a gradually secularizing world through simplification and return to its roots (as understood by the reformers), through purification of society, and by emphasis on faith and will to make faith a force even as outer conditions change.

It seems to be a law, of a piece with the overall irreversibility of historical time, that once a certain response has been massively implemented in a Great Religion's history, it cannot be tried again in the same way, no more than one can step into the same river twice or return to an earlier stage of one's life. Later we shall speculate on whether Christianity could undergo a second reformation, though one based on a different central focus than the justification by faith of the last; this would be as close as one might come to a repetition of a religion's history. More broadly speaking, once history is discovered it becomes a part of the human way of being in the world, and there is no stopping its momentum. In time, then, all the responses to historical circumstances, and to its internal needs, that are possible within a religion's finite potential, as defined by its identifying structures, are exhausted.

The legitimacy of such a view of history based on predictable stages needs to be addressed. From Hegel and Marx to Spengler and Toynbee, those who have subjected history to schematization and stages have played to mixed reviews. Like the earlier Joachim of Flora and the late prophets of a "Greening of America" and an Aquarian Age, they have in the end usually been seen as revealing more about the hopes and fears of their own age than about the veiled future. As we have seen, such schemes can also easily be identified (though I think not quite accurately) with the Grand Narratives condemned by postmodernists.

Nonetheless, the pattern of stages in the history of a Great Religion advanced here differs from the foregoing by depending on no grand mystical idea of meaning in history or the evolution of Absolute Spirit, but on rational, empirical observations of how religions work, and by extrapolation will work, in historical time. They are generalizations, to be sure, and to this extent hypotheses, but they are based on a reading of history and not a priori theories.

Finally, for those who have ears to hear it in this way, I would like for this scheme to be received as a prophetic utterance in the biblical sense: a prediction of the future of religion as it will be if forces in motion continue to work themselves out, but a future that can be changed if enough people want it changed and decide to change it. I am not a historical determinist; I believe persons and groups can take decision that can make the future whatever they wish it to be. But I also believe that the social forces constructing history are powerful and will not change unless they are opposed with great conviction and force. To stand against the tide is difficult for an individual, and more so for a group or nation, but it has been and can be done.

Many people both East and West will undoubtedly be distressed by the indication in the schema that Buddhism is about at its end as a Great Religion. First let it be emphasized that this does not mean there will be no more Buddhists; only that the religion will no longer have the Great Religion role on the world stage as in its golden age. To Buddhists one could say (a) that the diminishment of the faith in this age of the world is only what has been long predicted in Buddhist doctrines of the decline of the Dharma, and (b) that Buddhists can decide to perpetuate their religion as long as they wish to do so. Such "decisions," contrary to what would seem historically "natural," have been made before. Shinto, as a religion of a basically archaic agricultural type, should perhaps have given way entirely when the Great Religions Buddhism and Confucianism came to Japan, as did its polytheistic equivalents, the pre-Christian religions of Europe and the Mediterranean, before the rise of Christianity. But Japan collectively "decided" to preserve the older indigenous faith alongside the continental imports, and it is still there. The tenacity of Judaism almost everywhere it has spread in the face of immense pressure is well known and can surely serve as an inspiration to all who wish, despite great adversity, to preserve an ancient faith. As we have hinted with talk of a second Christian reformation, I suspect some future Christians will feel this way about their faith. But "preserved" religions may, in the end, find themselves as small a percentage of the human race as are Jews or Shintoists today.

Nonetheless, let the prophecies of this book be taken in the spirit with which all prophecy in a nondeterministic world must be taken, as saying: if things remain as they are, this will happen. But if we decide to change the present, the future will also change.

We shall now examine the stages of the historical development of the Great Religions, according to our hypothesis. We may recall that each stage *averages* some five centuries, but in practice each individual stage has varied as much as three or four centuries from that norm.

Apostolic Stage

This first stage covers the lifetime of the founder of the religion and its first few generations. It is pre-Constantinian Christianity,

Buddhism before Ashoka, Confucianism in the "Hundred Philosophers" era before its adoption by the Han dynasty as an official ideology, Hinduism in its formative period before the Gupta dynasty, Islam—in which the period was very short—prior to the caliphate.

Several distinctive characteristics mark this beginning phase. The new religion is a gestating faith, sometimes persecuted and precarious, dwelling within the womb of an older spiritual culture. It represents an alternative to it that may well look less "religious" and more concerned with this-worldly problem solving than what is spiritually around it. This is because the new faith has not yet taken up an elaborate metaphysical world view, but is instead a set of new techniques and simple principles that deal with what are widely, if perhaps only half consciously, perceived to be the "real" life problems of the times, to which the older spirituality's approach is anachronistic. The new faith's appeal, despite its socially and politically marginal status, rests in this perception. The older religion is richer in gods, philosophy, rituals, and piety and commands no small respect, but yet it is too cosmic and mystical to fit where people really feel they are at the current benchmark of the Axial Age.

Early Buddhism was more a pared-down psychotherapy than the equivalent of the Brahmanical rites and thought of its day. Confucianism was more an ethical and political system that kept the gods of the older cults at a distance. Hinduism in its corresponding period in the first centuries of the common era, in contrast to the by then culturally powerful but increasingly metaphysical Buddhism, presented a face of greater concern with the practical issues of a religiously legitimated social order, as in the Laws of Manu and the Bhagavad-Gita. Early Christianity was an experience of salvation and a relatively austere ethic, still feeling its way toward full theological exposition. Early Islam was as much a powerful political movement as a religion, greatly concerned with the regulation of life in this world. The apostolic religion, in other words, deals with the problem of the isolated, historically aware individual in the Axial Age, but not so much by offering him or her a full-sailed metaphysical bark, as by providing—in the Buddhist term—a ferry to the other shore, which is sturdy but simple, takes some effort to row, and gives a journey with this-worldly as well as otherworldly benefit.

"Early Islamic Dynasties." Illustration from the *Zabdat al-tawarikh* (Cream of Chronologies), Turkish, ca. 1600. Reprinted by permission of the Chester Beatty Library, Dublin.

A religion in an apostolic period is in a state of considerable flux as it finds its way from charismatic to routinized hierarchical leadership and hammers out its norms of doctrine and practice. What will later seem heretical extremes, such as Gnostic Christianity and Hsun-tzu's naturalistic Confucianism, may appear briefly as options for the direction the faith will take, and indeed may be covertly incorporated into its mature form. Three overriding drives, however, will become increasingly apparent as the period draws to a close: desires for institutional stability, doctrinal consensus, and political legitimation.

Religionists thereby acknowledge that the initial enthusiasm cannot succeed in conquering the world, or even in long sustaining itself, without conceptual and institutional unity, and support from a powerful state, which the faith in turn undergirds spiritually.

By the end of the apostolic period the new religion usually has shaken out a stable, working institutional and leadership pattern, whether under bishops, caliph, or monastic order. It is probably already in the process of producing the definitive version of the scriptures, and less formally of theological definition. The apostolic age comes to an end as two things happen, usually more or less simultaneously: the adoption of the faith by a powerful empire (Ashoka's, Han China, the Gupta dynasty, Constantine's, the caliphate), and the establishment of doctrinal agreement by the faith's institutional leadership aligned with the imperial patron. Often this consensus is reached by formal council, such as Nicaea and the other Christian general councils or the early Buddhist councils. Or a parallel process may be followed, such as the production of the definitive edition of the Koran under the third caliph, Uthman, and the "seeking of the Hadith," a systematic locating of the Prophet's words and acts to form the basis of Islamic law, a task completed by the end of the third century after his death. To become a Great Religion, a faith needs a political and geographical base of imperial dimensions, an authoritative institution, and a received scripture, as well as the rest of a religion's forms of expression. Those that have attained this highest destiny have, by the terminus of the first of their five eras, consolidated those requisites or are well on the way to securing them.

Wisdom and Imperial Stage

This stage represents what becomes of a Great Religion when it acquires that imperial alliance and becomes dominant in a major society and culture area for the first time. Its attitudes, praxis, and institutional life must adjust to meet this role. Becoming a "church" in the Troeltschean sense, it endeavors to maintain its integrity while making countless adaptations to meet the spiritual expectations of people from peasants to philosophers and emperors, people who are moreover of varying cultural background.

The religion must be new, to indicate that in it a new spiritual era has arrived; and old, to show that it is disarmingly only the fulfillment of what has gone before. While establishing its unquestioned spiritual supremacy through a hierarchy, an imposing institutionalism, and a political alliance, the newly triumphant faith borrows and assimilates rites and ideas from its environment with a free hand. It now needs with acute urgency not only symbols of continuity, but the full panoply of popular religion to meet all that is expected of a dominant faith: seasonal festivals, pilgrimage sites, imposing rituals, the ceremonies of sacred kingship, wayside shrines, charms and amulets. Some of this the austere monks and apostles of the earlier age might have scorned, but because it is an age when many kinds of religious language still speak, the religion cannot do otherwise without losing all viability at the moment of its greatest apparent success. The emergent new shapes are opposed only by a minority of purists, some of whom may express their protest by becoming ascetics or sectarians. This was also the age when Christian monasticism, Islamic Sufism, and various rigorist "heresies" appeared.

By and large, though, the religion's initial emphasis on a pivotal event in history, the foundation of its initial missionary proclamations, is now considerably softened by reversion to cosmic, sacred-and-profane patterns. On the popular level, festivals such as the Christian Christmas and Easter, though retaining their historical reference in principle, go far toward becoming eternal-recurrence seasonal rites in effect. Rites of regular worship such as the mass and the Muslim Friday prayers in the mosque or Buddhist temple offerings lost their original sharp sense of commemorating one who once lived in historical time and died a human death, to focus rather on his timeless mode of existence and to evoke it through the creation of sacred space and time, day after day or week after week.

Intellectually the same is reflected in a trend that gives this stage part of its name, an increasing appeal to the motif of universal wisdom rather than to the more historical and existential dimensions of the faith's early years. The historical task is, for the moment, accomplished with the emergence of an empire of believers. The religion's social program must now be to move that empire out of history, as it were, to become an unchanging, because now fulfilled, reflection of timeless reality, under a ruler who, like the Byzantine or Chinese emperor or the caliph in Baghdad, is Son of Heaven or Shadow of God, whose obligation is to innovate nothing but to preserve all things as ordained from above.

Philosophically, the corresponding trend is toward ideas and literature that grow more out of mystical and less from salvation experience, and that minimize the unique historicity of the religion in favor of its primordial and universal truth. Older and probably more universalistic conceptual motifs will be brought into the service of the new truth, at the same time tilting it in their direction. In the end, the new religion, though triumphant in name, will be intellectually a subtle synthesis of old philosophy and new doctrine.

In Chinese religion, this is the "Han synthesis" version of Confucianism, associated with Tung Chung-shu (ca. 179–104 B.C.E.), which incorporated Taoist and other traditional motifs into the thought of the Great Sage and his lineage with a generous hand, making it more metaphysical, imbued with doctrines of correspondences interweaving man and nature, and fashioning as Confucian rites those by which the emperor conformed his practices to the turning seasons.

In Buddhism, this is the era of the rise of Mahayana thought, with its universalistic emphasis on the universal Buddhahood of all beings rather than the historical Buddha, and in which Prajnaparamita, the "Wisdom That Has Gone Beyond," often worshiped as an initiatory goddess, was an important feature. The extent to which the wisdom of the new religion is but a revamping of old wisdom in the culture is shown by the obvious links between Mahayana and Upanishadic/Vedanta thought.

Yet Hinduism, in its own wisdom era as a Great Religion, if we take its inception as such to be around the first century C.E., was in turn influenced by Mahayana Buddhism. This is the Hinduism of the Gupta empire (fourth–sixth centuries C.E.), often regarded as the golden age of classical Hindu civilization. Then Hinduism, no doubt partly responding to the challenge of Buddhist thought, saw the crystallization of philosophical Vedanta, a highly mystical and universalistic philosophy stressing the presence of the One, Brahman, in all things, a realization attained by mystical experience. It was also the age of the Puranas, mythological texts, but often not without considerable theological insight, through which the culti of great populations were brought into formal Hinduism through the identification of their gods and myths with those of the Great Tradition.

In Christianity, we are of course speaking of patristic theology and its era. The Greek and Latin Fathers greatly stressed such timeless, universalistic aspects of the faith as the Trinity and the eternal Logos incarnate in Christ over against historical particularism. The liturgy also, both Eastern and Western, became a hieratic service that seemed less the memorial of a historical event than an eternally recurring breakthrough of the timeless, paradisal realm of the Trinity and the saints into time. Society, seeking to become Augustine's *Civitas Dei,* pursued, despite extremely tumultuous conditions on the worldly plane, models of perfection rather than historical destinies.

In Islam, this is the five centuries of the Baghdad and Cordova caliphates, a cultural golden age when Islamic philosophy, drawing from the Greek heritage and the experience of Sufi mysticism, reacted against Mu'tazili rationalism and the dry legalism of exoteric Islam to stress the timeless character of both God and the Koranic revelation, culminating in the inward universalism of al-Ghazzali and Ibn Arabi.

The imperial and wisdom era, then, fully establishes the Great Tradition of a Great Religion in both its social and intellectual dimensions, placing an elite of thinkers and hierarchs in powerful positions at courts royal and imperial, and as well in monasteries and universities. These persons go to great lengths to orient the

"Shiva Dancing on the Body of Tripoura-Soura." Reprinted by permission of the Musée Guimet.

new religion toward the whole accessible heritage of culture and thought. By the same token, the religion almost spontaneously creates popular forms that admit peasant masses into its ambit, retailing the faith on the level of folklore and village temples. But the culture-shaping, feeling-enhancing potential of a rising Great Religion are not exhausted by the structures of the second stage.

Devotionalism Stage

The assimilative imperial and wisdom stage gradually issues in another, with a fresh set of attitudes and central practices. This is the devotionalism broadly associated with the Middle Ages in most of the great faiths. The image of the person capable of giving and receiving love is its keynote, embracing both divine personalities and their human devotees. Love thus becomes both the supreme symbol of the divine and the locus of the human relationship with ultimate reality. The word *symbol* is used here in the Tillichian sense of that which participates in what it symbolizes. Devotionalism emphasizes personality—the personal as capable of distinctive traits of character, of giving and receiving love, of acting spontaneously and unexpectedly, of manifesting what is really most important about the Transcendent.

By the same token, devotion emphasizes that it is the person with these qualities who best worships God; what God treasures most in his lovers is the spontaneous gesture of unconditional love, such as the offering of the juggler of Notre Dame, marked by the unique personality of the worshiper.

Thus, whereas in the wisdom stage of Christianity the human personality of Christ was all but eclipsed by assimilating him to such more abstract roles as universal Logos and Pantocrator, in the Middle Ages, after the devotional stage had well set in, his lovable personhood—if not exactly his personality in the modern sense—returned as Saint Francis, according to significant tradition, made the first Christmas crèche and there worshiped divinity contained in infant flesh, and Saint Bernard sang, "Jesus, the very thought of Thee, with sweetness fills the breast."

Devotionalism is profoundly reflected in art. Indeed, in most places this is the greatest hour of religious architecture and iconography. The exaltation of sacred personhood and sacred feeling within the worshiper naturally calls forth the greatest efforts of artists, by which all their skills can be unleashed to reveal the tenderness, the mystery, and the individual uniqueness of gods, buddhas, saints, and saviors.

Intellectually, this age represents a culmination of the great system-making program implicit in the previous stage, when all of nature and supernature, all the orders human and divine, are brought together in vast enterprises of the mind that show their interconnectedness: the *Summa* of Thomas, the Buddhist syntheses of Tientai and Shingon. The relation of these Great Tradition works to devotionalism may not be immediately apparent, yet it is there, for they provide the overall legitimation for the particularistic roles of objects of devotion by appropriately placing them in the hierarchy of heaven and earth or the stages of the spiritual life. Then gods, buddhas, or saints can step out of the mandala or the latinate pages of theology to bless or answer heartfelt prayer, their place intuitively grasped by the simple and understood by the wise.

Politically, this is a time when the imperial unity of the second stage has tended to give way to a number of feudal states within the religion's orbit, though the memory of empire remains potent. This abets tendencies toward religious particularism while emphasizing the religion's inherent universalism as the faith of many kingdoms. The plurality of paths and local manifestations that devotionalism makes evident opens deep currents leading toward the fragmentation of the next stage, while the universalist side will become fulfilled in the same stage's missionary impulse. In the devotional stage the faith also tends to become intermixed with knightly codes of chivalry.

The devotional stage is, then, the Christendom of 1000 to 1500 with its personal piety to Jesus, the Blessed Virgin, and the saints. This devotion was linked to the spirit of chivalry in aristocratic secular society and is reflected in warm and soaring Christian art from the great cathedrals to Giotto.

Devotionalism is Hindu bhakti in the same period, the great era of Hindu temple building, as it was of cathedral building in Europe. Though the roots of bhakti go back centuries before, its great age was from the composition of the Puranas in the early centuries of the common era to the time of Chaitanya (1485–

1533). Devotionalism reached its richest intellectual expression in the theology of Ramanuja (ca. twelfth century), was popularized by poets from the Alvars to Kabir, and inspired the great temples and sculpture of Hindustan.

In Buddhism it is the period 500 to 1000, which under the powerful influence of such texts as the Lotus Sutra, saw the rise of devotion to such buddhas and bodhisattvas as Avalokitesvara (Japanese Kannon), Kshitigarba (Japanese Jizō), and above all Amitabha (Japanese Amida) of the presectarian Pure Land Buddhism gathering strength in China and Japan. It was also the period when, in Buddhist India, Tibet, and parts of southeast Asia, the very different but also personalized and experiential Vajrayana took shape, with its emphasis on evocational meditation spilling over into incomparable art. From Borobodur in Java to the Hōryūji in Japan, many of the greatest of Buddhist temples derive from this era. Perhaps its most characteristic expression, however, and the one that marks it as Buddhism's devotional stage, was the Tientai school attributed to Chih-i (538–97), which was to be so important for Buddhism's next, reformation stage. Tientai afforded an immense umbrella under which innumerable noncompetitive forms of devotion to buddhas and bodhisattvas could be arrayed.

For Chinese religion generally, the same period (or more precisely, from the fall of the Han dynasty in 220 to the rise of the Sung in 960 c.e.) represents the devotional stage. It includes the confused but culturally creative Three Kingdoms and Six Dynasties periods, when Buddhism and Taoism flourished, and the great T'ang era. This was an age of the relative recession of Confucianism, and appropriately of the heyday of personalistic, feeling-oriented Taoist and Chinese Buddhism traditions, with their hierarchies of gods, saviors, and immortals; their splendid art; and their popular devotionalism.

In Islam, the devotional period might be said to run from the time of Jalal al-Din Rumi (1207–73)—whose incomparable poetry and whose Sufi order, the first, opened an unprecedented popular enthusiasm for the Sufi's mystical and devotional Islam—to the beginning of the twentieth century, when the tide of that expression of Islam began to recede before the gathering forces of the Islamic reformation.

What are some reasons devotionalism takes over from the imperial-wisdom expression of a Great Religion?

First, as a faith still relatively new to a society in the second stage puts down deeper and deeper roots, sinking into folklore and folk custom, its popular forms naturally become stronger and more self-confident. In the nature of things, these expressions are likely to have proto-devotional characteristics, or practices such as offerings and pilgrimage, which can easily take on the emotional coloring of devotionalism. By the religion's third stage, these forms will have worked their way up again to acquire Great Tradition sanction and a patina of great art and poetry to set the tone of an entire period.

Second and concomitantly, as a religion's expression in art and literature matures, it almost inevitably becomes less archetypally stylized and more person centered, evoking as does all sophisticated work the many cloaks of the human and the divine. Great personalizing religious art creates as well as reflects the devotional mood, from the wonderfully human yet transcendent buddhas of Nara to the imbibers of mystical wine in Persian miniatures.

Third and above all, devotionalism reflects the religionists' burgeoning confidence in themselves as persons. This is the result of the religion's having finally created a fairly stable and self-confident culture in the imperial and wisdom stage. Its struggles for spiritual and political-social legitimation are now over; it has won. Its people can take themselves seriously as centers of feeling and meaning.

Yet devotionalism also reflects something opposite, the crisis of defining personhood in a period when outward society is likely to be slowly fragmenting following the imperial age. Thus Christian devotionalism arose in the wake of Byzantine and Carolingian imperial-wisdom Christianities, Hindu bhakti in the wake of the Gupta state (which also encouraged it), Muslim in the aftermath of the caliphate, Chinese of the Han, Buddhist of its Mauryan and Kushan patrons, among other imperial friends.

For reasons of both confidence and fragmentation, then, the self discovers that it can stand on its own before God or Ultimate Reality as a center of feeling, deciding, knowing inwardly, and loving, qualities that God and his lovers can mirror between each other. But the process has opened an inner floodgate that will not rest till its waters have washed with still more power over the fields of history.

Reformation Stage

The age of devotion culminates in a movement and era we may call reformation. It is a period averaging five centuries, the same as the others: for though the revolutionary upheaval itself may be relatively brief, a matter of decades or at most a generation or two, it establishes the religion's character and agenda for the next several centuries.

The reformation era is a complex period. Spiritually it has roots in devotionalism, for among its salient features are simplification of focus and emphasis on inwardness, which the previous era had encouraged. In a sense it is a reverse of the wisdom period's interpretation of the religion, for where the latter had moved toward timeless and universal realities, the reformation narrows its expansiveness down to simple, personal issues in crucial respects. If an age is often better understood by the questions it asks than the answers it gives, wisdom asks, and the scholastic wing of devotion further asks, "How can all the entities of the universe and human experience, including the facts of the new faith, be integrated into an immense interlocking system?" But reformation inquires, with Luther, "How can I be sure that I am saved?"

Nonetheless, religion still has considerable capital to expend in the era of reformation. It may shift direction, but it remains an immensely powerful historical force. Though the emergence of the reformation age is itself basically the product of the religion's own internal dynamics, those same dynamics now begin to tilt the balance more and more toward responding to external historical change as well. Although of course it benefited from political alliances and incorporated much from outside in the second and third stages, still the new Great Religion set its spiritual tone from out of its own essence and was fundamentally in charge. Now we see the cutting edge of spiritual and cultural change occasionally slip from its grasp, though the Great Religion retains plenty of fight, and battle is joined. Yet the battle itself has at least half the nature of response.

If the wisdom and devotional periods represent the classical eras of a religion, its moments of triumph and culture creation, reformation is its first great reaction to a changing world—a response, or rather series of responses, made when the religion still has power to respond on the Great Tradition level, as equal to anything else in the intellectual, educational, political, economic, and artistic worlds at their best. But now it is not the *only* entity in those worlds and is itself increasingly divided.

The first obvious stage setting for reformation is likely to be, as the devotion period draws to an end, the rise of national governments that lack the intimate relation to the religion of predecessors, though no doubt they nominally support it if of the same faith. This phenomenon is itself the product of historical forces related to the rise of the Great Religion. Very rare is the human empire, dynasty, or political order that lasts more than two or three hundred years; even rarer that which, so enduring, does not undergo major modification. By now the empire that first harbored the nascent religion and put it on the world stage is long since gone, and so are the successor states, which, at least initially, probably emulated its policies toward the faith.

Certain of the present states are likely to be less congenial toward the religion for three reasons. First, as the shadow of the past fades, the new states wish less to view themselves as perpetuators of the old holy society, with its alliance of throne and altar, and instead to develop new policies exploring other options, such as greater independence of state from church.

Second, the religion, now 1500 years old, has said much, codified much, searched out the ramifications of its lore very far. It has, without substantial change in its angle of vision, less and less truly new to say, though new conditions have inevitably appeared on earth. Some secularization appears by default as the religion finds it impossible both to remain consistent with its accumulated past and to respond as flexibly as it could a thousand years earlier.

Third, as the wheel of history turns, it is likely that some areas in which the population is of one Great Religion will be ruled by a conquering elite of another, as was Hindu India by the Mughuls. This naturally means that even the Great Tradition of the popular faith has only limited rapport with the state. This relative aliena-

Buddha, Sarnath, Archaeological Museum. Photograph by Jean-Louis Nou. Reprinted by permission of Herder Verlag, from Jeannine Auboyer, *Buddha* (New York: Crossroad, 1983).

tion of religion and government will have a "spillover" in incipient alienation of religion from other pillars of society, such as education, economic life, and art. These in their own way become more secular in content and style as the state becomes less interested in patronizing exclusively religious activities, and the court sets an example of comparatively worldly sophistication.

So it is that on the eve of their reformation eras, we find Buddhism and Chinese religion under Kamakura and Sung regimes fairly unsympathetic to traditional patterns of relation between religion and the state, though holding many supporters open to new spiritual prospects—Hinduism in an India increasingly subject to Muslim rule; Christianity in a Europe of nationalism and nation-states alive with new ideas and restive under feudal ecclesiastical and political patterns; and Islam early in the twentieth century subjected either to colonial rule by Christian powers or to anachronistic regimes such as the Ottoman and Persian empires, also dominated in numerous ways from the European capitals.

Yet, as indicated, religion still had the energy to respond powerfully and creatively to this situation. Its fundamental perception at this point was that the faith must rediscover what its essentials are and press them to the exclusion of all else. The "essentials" will naturally be sought in the context of devotionalism, the motif of the era now passing away. They are therefore likely to be at least in part faith and feeling oriented, to hold that true religion means right subjectivity, an inner simplification around that within which is most in touch with the divine. But the reformation quest will go beyond devotionalism in two ways: it will strive to focus faith on a single object and emphasize simple acts of faith, thereby cutting through the imagistic and emotional complexity characteristic of devotionalism; and it may in some places attempt to create an ideal religious society, bringing back under religious control political and economic areas of life that seemed in danger of slipping away, as in Calvin's Geneva or the Islamic Republic of Iran.

The reformation response, then, is basically one of simplification, of seeking a single simple sure key to the heart of the religion that makes it available anywhere, to anyone, in a changing world, and attempting to make it relevant—whether through social control or inward application—in all arenas of life. The search for a single simple sure key will often mean a deliberate effort to "return to the sources," to concentrate on what are believed to be the crucial texts and doctrines and practices, rejecting all else much more rigorously than before. The ideal is to recover the primitive or ideal form of the faith, inevitably presumed to have been simpler than what it has become in the present degenerate times.

Simplification is bound to mean that the faith is relatively laicized, popularized, and turned toward the importance of right subjectivity in the form of emphasis on faith and lay "inner asceticism" in principle. For simplification down to a single sure key makes it more and more accessible to everyone, whether specialist or not. Nonetheless, a Great Tradition type of elite continues in practice to dominate the intellectual and institutional life of the reformed faith, though it may be an elite of a different structure than before. Yet the simplification does make spiritual life more congenial to participation in "ordinary" life in a world seen as increasingly secularized; priesthood and monasticism and elaborate rites appropriate to specialists are devalued, though charismatic leadership is not.

Reformation leads to a process of development in the religion lasting half a millennium. Here are a few characteristics.

First, we must make the important observation that reform usually begins and takes its classic institutional form only in one part of the religion's world. That place will be on its periphery from the perspective of the religion's place of origin and traditional centers of power, a place missionized only fairly late in its expansion, and of a varying language and culture—Japan for Buddhism, Bengal for Hinduism, Germanic northern Europe for Christianity, Iran for Islam. Only the Chinese Neo-Confucian reformation, of a somewhat different nature, did not have a clear geographical focus.

The bulk of the religion, outside that place, will be affected only indirectly by reformation, through reaction against it, as with Counter-Reformation Catholicism, or through a gradual, diffuse influence. But from this point on the reformation forms of the religion will represent its intellectual and historical edge. At the very beginning of the reformation, as we have seen, it—or perhaps sectarian forms—may endeavor to establish an ideal society. But as these efforts inevitably fail, the religion settles into a comfortable relation with society. Yet it is still yeasty, capable of fresh and energetic ventures both in its reform and counter-reform wings.

In the middle or late reformation period the religion will show an upsurge of expansiveness and missionary activity—the potent spread of Neo-Confucianism to Korea and Japan; the evangelism of Pure Land, Nichiren, and Zen Buddhism in Japan and even beyond; in Hinduism the Bengal-based rise of such movements as the Ramakrishna Mission and the exportation of the faith to the West; in Christianity the great nineteenth-century missionary movement.

Toward the end of the reformation period there comes a trend toward theological liberalism, interpreting the religion in fairly relativistic, naturalistic ways believed to be compatible with the best current secular or scientific world views—the naturalistic Buddhism of Ashikaga and Momoyama Japan (Yoshida Kenkō, the Zen of Higashiyama culture, later Bankei); the ideology of the nineteenth-century "Hindu renaissance" (Roy, Vivekananda, Radhakrishnan); Christian liberalism from Schleiermacher to Tillich. Understandably, liberalism produces conservative reactions, but liberalism—and the strongest of the reactions, such as those of Aurobindo or Barth—represent the last great intellectual effort of the faith.

Finally, we may note that at the close of the reformation era, its values tend to spread through the whole of the religion, though often in partial and unacknowledged form. The Hindu reformism of Gandhi and Bhave diffused such ideals of reformation bhakti as simple faith and transcendence of caste; Roman Catholicism after Vatican II is certainly more "protestant" than before. It may be pointed out that at the very end of the reformation period a sort of resurgence of energy often arises; it may seem to be a rebirth, but may really be more of an afterglow. It represents the last period when the religion and society, including the intellectual establishment, interact on more or less equal terms. One thinks of religion and the independence movement in Hindu India, or the theological renaissance of the first half of the twentieth century in Christianity.

In Buddhism, the reformation period is basically that inaugurated by the new Kamakura period movements in Japan, Pure Land, Nichiren, and Zen in its Japanese form. These represented a return to simple textual and experiential sources (the Pure Land texts, the Lotus Sutra, direct experience), popularization, and the use of a single simple sure key to salvation accessible to everyone: faith in Amida Buddha, the Nichiren *daimoku* chant, Zen sitting. As in Europe, the relative laicization and simplification of religion in the reformation had a clear relation to the emergence of a powerful mercantile and later industrial class in Japan.

In Chinese religion, the reformation was the emergence of Neo-Confucianism in the relatively secular Sung era (960–1279); it became state orthodoxy in the Ming (1368–1644) and thereafter. In interaction with Buddhism and Taoism, but also in response to needs for simplification and inwardness in a society growing more complex, Neo-Confucianists put emphasis on the inward state of mind of the sage, on settling one's mind and so seeing the *li,* or principles of things. The movement took on popular religious forms in mass meetings with lectures on self-cultivation and in the stress, particularly in the Wang Yang-ming school of Neo-Confucianism, on the "Three Teachings"—Confucianism, Taoism, and Buddhism—as coequal Chinese traditions and ways of self-realization.

The Hindu reformation began in Bengal with the Chaitanya Krishnaite movement of the sixteenth century, emphasizing pure simple faith and worship toward Krishna, deemphasizing brahmanical rites and caste, and making inward fervor compatible with life in the world as a believer. Some of the same subjective and social themes, though now from an Advaita Vedanta rather than bhakti perspective, were revived in the nineteenth-century Hindu modernization movements centering in Bengal: the Brahmo Samaj, the Ramakrishna Mission, and their kin. The reformation's last great outburst was in the reform and independence movement of Gandhi and his followers, which was deeply grounded in religion.

As Max Weber pointed out long ago, India did not have a reformation with the same economic consequences as the European, or one might add the Buddhist in Japan. This was largely because India was dominated by alien rulers during most of the reformation era, whether Muslim or British. But it must be recognized that there was an ideological movement in the Hindu world beginning around 1500, which led, like the European reformation, from inward faith to liberalism and social change, while maintaining dialogue but not identity with other major social institutions.

The outline of the Protestant Reformation in Christianity is well known. One point that might be noted is the sense in which this reformation, like all such, brought a radical pluralization of the religion's forms of expression and an acceleration of its history. Despite some sectarian movements, for its first 1500 years Christianity, both Eastern and Western, maintained a generally Catholic image, hierarchical and sacramental, which gave it a reasonably consistent identity throughout time and the Christian world. Only a relatively few forms of Christian expression were heavily utilized.

Then, suddenly by historical standards, an astonishing array of new forms of expression appeared, from the ornate shape of baroque Catholicism to Lutheran sermons and Quaker meetings, from Unitarian rationalism to pentecostal fire. In the same period both its inward drive and historical circumstances favored the religion's expansion, till it became the largest and most widespread faith the world had ever known.

What this portends for the future remains to be seen. One could argue that, like Buddhism and Chinese religion, it has run through a wide repertoire but one that in the end must be exhausted; that by doing so much in these five centuries it may have, like a bursting rocket, cast its brilliance and is now falling amid still glowing embers. Or it may be that this remarkable creativity suggests a future capacity as well to let new occasions teach new forms and new duties.

The Islamic reformation is just beginning, if our hypothesis is correct. Thus far, it is displaying many common characteristics of the period. There is a response to secularizing trends, an inward fervor, the early desire to create an ideal society, the emergence of a new kind of elite, a drive to return to the religion's source and simplify Islam to the practice of the Shari'ah, the fundamental law.

Folk Religion Stage

In its terminal stage a Great Religion continues, perhaps for several centuries, as little more than popular or folk religion. We

The Grotto at Lourdes. Reprinted by permission from *Mysteries of the World*, by Christopher Pick (London: Lyric Books Ltd., 1979).

shall later examine the nature of folk religion in more detail. Here it may suffice to indicate that we mean by it religious attitudes, practices, and institutions preserved in families and local communities, but having little rapport with the major structures of society or the mainstream of its thought and culture. It depends more on traditionalist and charismatic rather than rational authority; it is cosmic and feeling rather than history and mind oriented; it may involve some recovery of devotionalist and even cosmic religion motifs as reformation simplification loses its sharpness.

The sort of radical change and acceleration suggested by reformation in interaction with the emergence of a new kind of society has thus far happened only once on a large scale in a Great Religion's history. After that upheaval, as new social changes occur, the religion seems slowly to lose touch with the major structures of society—political, economic, educational, cultural. It therefore meets less well than before the real trends of the society and the psyches of individuals therein. Unable to reverse this distancing, having exhausted its intellectual and creative potential, it no longer attracts the sort of leadership that could keep alive its Great Tradition. Yet it can long continue on the popular level in favorable circumstances, for reasons we shall consider later.

This stage may not, however, be fully understood, for only two examples have arisen so far, Chinese religion since the beginning of the Ch'ing period (1644) and Buddhism since around the same point. Since the seventeenth century both religions have displayed little vigorous intellectual life or cultural creativity, and what there was of it, Hakuin's Zen or Kang Yu-wei's Confucianism, had none of the historical force of say Gandhi or Martin Luther King at the end of the Hindu or Christian reformation periods. Instead, the Chinese and Japanese governments of that period were generally as secular as any premodern regimes, using the vapid institutional religion of their societies as mere instruments of control; popular Taoist, Shinto, or bodhisattva cults flourished mightily, however, with great pilgrimages and frenzies. But art and literature were increasingly secular, as in the celebrated *ukiyo* ("floating world") prints and stories of Japan; and real intellectual life in both countries, and Korea, centered around philology and philosophy in the Confucian tradition but of little real religious content. In the Theravada Buddhist countries of Southeast Asia, Buddhist practice has remained vigorous, but there too little innovative

Buddhist intellectual or cultural energy has been visible in recent centuries.

Does the present state of religion actually confirm our five-stage hypothesis? To answer this question fully, and then to proceed with our argument, we need first to examine in some depth the debate over secularization. Is the alleged decline of religion in the modern world a clear reality, a learned illusion, or might not the facts—whatever they may be—also be amenable to interpretation through a third possibility, such as the working out of the stages in the lives of the Great Religions we have proposed?

Chapter 5

The Modern World and Secularization

To those who believe in secularization, the modern fall of religion from the privileged status it is alleged once to have had is a patent reality, the kind of thing "everyone knows." They often seem to respond to their critics with a hint of irritation that supposedly intelligent people should refuse obstinately to accept such an obvious fact, as though talking to a flat-earther. But on the other hand critics of secularization theory point to their own obstinate facts. They note religion's continuing prosperity in much of the modern world, its protean ability to take new forms and seize new opportunities as the world changes, its ability to exploit rather than retreat before the social and technological novelties of the twentieth century. Critics may query whether a theory which requires so many qualifications and superimposed epicycles to make it fit the facts as secularization may not be a sociological equivalent of ptolemaic astronomy.

Nevertheless, the idea of secularization persists. At least until recently, most significant sociologists and historians of religion have accepted it in some form. Indeed, if we follow Durkheim's reflections at the conclusion of *The Elementary Forms of the Religious Life*,[1] or the later observations of Bryan Wilson,[2] we must concede that secularization theory is built into the very nature of the sociological enterprise. For if, as the latter must assume, religion can be interpreted, in part or in whole, by sociological analysis, then that religion is dethroned as absolute monarch and subjected to a higher law. In Durkheimian parlance, if the real though unacknowledged object of religion is society itself, then religious knowledge can be replaced by sociological knowledge, and must be when the latter arrives on the scene. The sociologist by the very act of sociologizing also secularizes, and insofar as his or her work has any impact on the attitudes of society as a whole, secularization is furthered.

The fathers of sociology, from Comte, Durkheim, and Weber on down, assumed in principle the truth of Peter Berger's definition of secularization as "the process by which sectors of society and culture are removed from the domination of religious institutions and symbols," together with its subjective corollary, the "secularization of consciousness."[3] They then proceeded to explain how and why this removal has come to pass, and to deal with questions of to what extent religion has a future. Here differences have arisen.

The role of religion in society has been studied basically from two sociological perspectives. One, stemming from Emile Durkheim, has emphasized its origin in society itself and its role of giving cohesion to society. Religion provides the myths, rituals, values, and sense of identity that bind a community together on the level of symbol and feeling, inducing members to make pro-community choices.

The other, grounded in the work of Max Weber, stresses what may be called the cognitive and operational aspects of religion: its way of providing knowledge of the supernatural and of managing human response to it, or manipulation of it. For Weber this knowledge and power was primarily transmitted to and through individuals—charismatic persons, magicians, priests—rather than residing in a Durkheimian social effervescence. But of course its social impact, as well as its indirect origin in societal problems and needs, is pervasive. The exploration of that interrelationship was Weber's abiding concern.

The Durkheimian and Weberian approaches are not necessarily inconsistent, and most subsequent work in the sociology of religion has drawn from both. But each maintains a different emphasis in the understanding of religion with immense bearing on the problem of secularization. We shall examine each in turn, beginning with the Durkheimian.

If religion rests in the cohesion of society, its health depends on the extent to which society coheres, and likewise the extent to which religious symbols and acts reinforce this cohesion without people being aware that it is society, rather than transcendent religious realities, that is the true object of religious feeling. An extreme Durkheimian could argue that if society is the true focus of religion, then as long as there is society religion will persist, since all societies by definition have some kind of unifying symbol and structure. This proposition has led to some rather quixotic theories suggesting that seemingly secular means of social bonding, from Maoism in China (before the reaction against the Great Cultural Revolution) to the spirit of American pragmatism, are "really" religious despite the lack of a supernatural referent.

Although this approach obviously illumines important functional continuities, it makes the definition of religion so elastic as to render the word less useful than it ought to be. In light of religion's historic meanings, those concerned with public awareness of supernatural realities, one would expect to see in something properly called religion that awareness conveyed simultaneously through, say, Joachim Wach's three forms of religious expression—the theoretical, practical, and sociological.[4] In this vein Peter Berger has criticized Thomas Luckmann's interesting argument in *The Invisible Religion:* that religion is any universe of meaning human beings create to manifest their capacity to transcend biological nature.[5] In effect, then, any social phenomenon becomes at least potentially religious. But, Berger contends, when modern science, for instance, becomes a form of religion, as it may under Luckmann's definition, the utility of the word is weakened. Berger prefers to limit religion to the positing of a *sacred cosmos,* an objective moral-spiritual order legitimated by supernatural reality, by the sacred in something like Rudolf Otto's or Mircea Eliade's sense.[6] Under this definition we can take note of the countless permutations the sacred, in its dialectic with the profane, is able to take; but at the same time the possibility of true secularization, the disappearance of the sacred altogether, cannot be excluded.

Peter Berger is Durkheimian insofar as he assumes as his base point the social construction of a sacred reality that unifies cosmos, society, and the individual into a seamless whole. He likewise perceives a progressive disruption of this primordial whole in history. It has roots as far back as the Old Testament and the

Reformation, and involves a "disenchantment of the world" in which demarcations are made between the sacred and the secular, with the former more and more pushed to some transcendent point beyond the confines of this world altogether, or restricted to "specialized" institutions such as the Christian Church.

This is, clearly, a social process of secularization, the negative of the modernist Grand Narrative, even though as Berger tried to show in *A Rumor of Angels* the experiential sources of religion have not necessarily dried up.[7] But they have become quite personal, privatized, and at best express themselves only in relativistic religious forms within a pluralistic situation; in a disenchanted world the Transcendent must be found in whatever fragmented bits and pieces it can, and only the most obdurate will to believe can sustain more than a functionally relativistic belief in the truth of each. The sacred canopy of old is shattered.[8]

An important aspect of the Durkheimian tradition is the civil religion discussion, associated with Will Herberg and Robert Bellah.[9] Despite the obviously fragmented pluralism of religion in the United States, these writers contend, that country has also known a common if attenuated religious expression centered on such doctrines as belief in a divine providence guiding the destiny of the nation, together with ceremonies and symbols of the state as a community with sacred meaning. These workings have counterbalanced the rampage of pluralism and saved something of the Durkheimian function.

However one evaluates it, though, civil religion has apparently not proved of adequate mettle to withstand the onslaughts of secularization. Herberg regarded it as little more than a pious facade, of little weight compared to the testimony of the traditional faiths. Bellah, who at first took its significance as an expression of shared values even in a pluralistic situation more seriously, has acknowledged that in recent decades it has become a "broken and empty shell."[10] If values unite Americans, they are now wholly secular, pragmatic ones, without even such a vestigial sacred canopy legitimating them as civil religion. In true Durkheimian fashion, when the social nature of the sacred is discovered, its days are numbered, and sociological knowledge has replaced religious truth.

The question of the future of religion in Durkheimian terms is, then, one of whether religion can persist when fragmented into bits strewn through a society still reasonably homogeneous in all respects but religion. For despite much talk of general fragmentation, it is clear that stable, advanced nations, such as the United States or those of Europe, are still largely unified in most important areas except religion. Indeed, owing to the effects of mass media and rapid transportation, they may be becoming more so. The government is not about to collapse, a complex and well-meshed economic system sends standard brands out to the remotest hamlet, people laugh and weep at the same TV series in Maine and California and Australia, and educational systems are turning out more and more identical products across the world as far as secular skills and attitudes are concerned. Computer programming and marketing are far more identical in Boston and Bombay than are Calvinism and Krishnaism.

Only religion, despite its occasional attempts to market comparable standard brands and to employ the same mass media, seems incapable of attaining a similar unity. It does not really unite supposedly one-religion countries such as Spain or Sweden anymore, much less, apart from the remnants of civil religion, a country such as the United States. Otherwise identical engineers may be agnostics or fundamentalists; clean-cut Catholics and Quakers may enjoy the same Disneyland rides or TV shows side by side. Perhaps it doesn't matter; on the other hand, it doesn't gel.

It may be, as Peter Berger tells us, "increasingly difficult to maintain the religious traditions as unchanging verity" in this situation.[11] Religious groups can only shore up their own particular subworld and hope that, as far as their universal validity is concerned, the civil religion golden rule of "No offense" is kept and no one will be so uncivil as to point out that, with respect to any reasonable claim to universal validity, with so many emperors trying to share the imperial vestments each individual sovereign at best dons only a few tatters.

Nonetheless, it is obvious that some powerful force, some slow inertia or nuclear bonding, is keeping religious consciousness awake and religious groups alive despite what in terms of Durkheimian sociology ought to look like a pretty desperate situation. Their social cohesion role dissipating (save as it still serves class or ethnic needs), their claim to ultimate truth called into question by the relativizing fact of pluralism, their inability to move toward the same sort of homogenization as the rest of American and other culture painfully obvious—what sort of hope can religious groups have? Yet they persist and even flourish. Is it in fact as perennially resilient folk religion? We shall return to this paradox.

First, however, let us turn to the Weberian tradition. Here, if religion is the knowledge and operation of supernatural realities, then its health depends on the extent to which this knowledge is credible and the institutions devoted to its transmission accepted as legitimate and able to adapt themselves to changing conditions.

Some Weberians paint a picture somewhat rosier for religion than is common in the contemporary Durkheimian camp, with its elegies for a sacred canopy. Talcott Parsons, for example, contends that religion has in fact adapted itself with some success. He acknowledges that when societies were simple, elements we might call religious and others we might not were fused together in a single web of meaning, as in Berger's sacred canopy. As societies grew more complex, "differentiation" set in, with religious and secular institutions assuming different functions. Indeed, religious and worldly components of the individual psyche came to be differentiated. But this process, which some might call secularization, does not necessarily mean that religion is becoming less significant. In a world of specialists, religious specialists may be as credible as any other. Indeed, the fact that religion is increasingly individualized, and in a pluralistic world a matter of individual choice, might well serve to make it more important to an individual as such than when it was a more or less automatic part of tribal life. Further, religion's moral influence on seemingly secular institutions such as business and politics in a nation with a religious heritage may be indirect, but cannot be discounted.[12]

Andrew Greeley, combining both Durkheimian and Weberian approaches, comes to a similar cautiously optimistic view. There will always be religion, he asserts, since society requires it on Durkheimian grounds. Although perhaps a society theoretically could cohere on nonreligious values, no empirical evidence exists for this happening satisfactorily. But Greeley also argues for Parson's differentiation theory and Berger's pluralism, affirming that the Durkheimian role can be played by differentiated, pluralistic religion in a complex society. Under modern conditions, when fragmentation is a "given" of human experience, it does not automatically disqualify religion in the eyes of most; Greeley responds to Berger's ruminations on this matter by pointing to the fact that it is precisely the countries where religion is most pluralistic or even polarized, such as Holland, Ireland, and the United States, that it is apparently healthiest. In the modern world, competition among religions is expected and, far from weakening faith, seems to keep it alive and alert.[13]

Another sociologist who is skeptical of secularization hypotheses, but who is somewhat hard to place theoretically, is David Martin. His basic theory of religion seems to be Weberian in that it is cognitive, having to do with an "orientation towards the world" that includes a "transcendent vision,"[14] which has an operative role parallel to that of science. But of his own theory of secularization, he says that "Durkheim provided the frame."[15]

Fundamentally, though, Martin has conducted a campaign of elegant rear-guard fencing against proponents of general secularization theories. He is not so unwise as to say there is nothing to secularization at all. In an essay on secularization and the arts, he discusses the common observation that the style and content of music and the visual arts has become progressively more secular since the Middle Ages. He contends that this is not necessarily a barometer of society generally, but its instances can all be given special explanations. The change and decay that all around he sees in this particular field is, he holds in good High Tory fashion, all to be blamed on the influence of French culture.

So far as secularization as a "unified syndrome of characteristics subject to an irreversible master-trend" is concerned, it is an illusion. He makes the usual arguments that the data are inconsistent and difficult to interpret, that even where religious participation can be shown to be declining, as in his own England, a "subterranean theology" of religious-type attitudes persists, and that secularizing sociologists are blinded to these things by their own arbitrary definitions and reductionistic assumptions about religion.[16]

Nonetheless, the man who once said that the word *secularization* "should be erased from the sociological dictionary"[17] later wrote a book titled *A General Theory of Secularization*. Here David Martin argues for a short-term, "highly empirical" use of the concept. Again the French Revolution and its ilk are blamed for what reality there may be to secularizing trends. The latter stem from a vicious cycle set in motion when religion and a substantial part of the population are polarized against each other, as was the Church and its largely reactionary supporters against the working class and liberal opinion in France during the revolutionary era, a gulf that, as is well known, long remained a deep cleavage in French society. This disaster is apt to occur when society and religion are first posited in "monopolistic" terms, as was Catholicism in France especially after the revocation of the Edict of Nantes; in countries such as Holland and the United States, where two or more faiths have long shared spiritual sway, the French experience is not likely to occur.[18] However oversimplified this interpretation of religious history (and of course I have oversimplified Martin's book-length presentation of it), its kernel of truth serves to reinforce Greeley's contention that secularization is spotty and often illusory, and that religious pluralism, far from being the firebrand and terminal symptom of secularization in the modern world, may actually be its antidote.

Martin's cautious and critical use of the secularization concept is continued in his *Dilemmas of Contemporary Religion*,[19] in which, looking to the short-term future of Western religion, he anticipates a weakening of the central core of Euro-American cultural life through liberal pluralism and critical skepticism, but expects this decay will be met at the periphery by ethnic and religious resistance.

One sociologist who has few doubts about the reality of the secularization process is Martin's fellow Briton Bryan Wilson.[20] As befits the Weberian tradition, Wilson is inclined to give more significance to changes in the cognitive than in the social role of religion. Here he sees little ground for hope that religion, in anything like its traditional form, will rise again. The real change the world is undergoing is not in formal religious belief or practice, but in regard for the supernatural, in everyday belief in miracles, witches, and the like. On this front the real underpinnings of mass religiosity are being cut away. Those "secular" theologians and their sociological allies who attempt to salvage a religion without the old-fashioned supernatural are too sophisticated by half and of little relevance to the true situation.

For Wilson, the sort of theory that says a modern man is "really" religious because he washes his car religiously every Sunday morning or finds his ultimate concern in loving his wife or mistress; or that views the modern miracle-free church as more than the residue of a dying heritage, is simply engaging in definitional sleight of hand. Religion, if it means anything, must mean a downright belief that the supernatural is real and impinges readily and often on ordinary human life. That belief, and behavior associated with it, has been steadily dissipated by science and the march of modernity, even in people who think of themselves as religious. Therefore religion has declined and secularization advanced.

Put this way, I suppose even the most ardent antisecularization theorist, after much hemming and hawing, would have to agree with Wilson, although anyone who has been around evangelical and charismatic circles can affirm that supernatural signs and wonders are still a good way from total decline even in the supposedly most advanced societies.

The inevitability of the process is advocated by Wilson in his response to a rambling, learned article by Daniel Bell. Bell argues eloquently, if not with particular originality, that religion does not die but changes.[21] Like others, he grants that a process of secularization occurs as religion retreats from various areas of public life, but insists that it is only pulling back to its invulnerable redoubt in the private sphere. Religion, Bell declares, can operate in the cultural and personal lives of persons without being socially functional or affected by changes in social structure. This is ultimately because it deals with perennial human questions and concerns for meaning that persist regardless of social change.

Wilson answers that religious attitudes do, in fact, follow changes in society, though perhaps with a time lag. Any view that culture and belief for the average person can be hermetically sealed off from what is going on in the society of which he or she is a part is hopelessly naive or elitist. Belief in hell, for example, has notably declined with the modern rise in living standards, as this world has become far less of a vale of tears than it once was for most. In the same way, private religion cannot forever survive a loss of public function or social reason for its world view. The questions of meaning may, of course, continue to be asked, but this does not mean they need to be put or answered in religious terms, which as we have seen would mean for Wilson supernatural terms.[22]

Despite such objections as these, others too have seen a future for religion in the personal arena. Huston Smith has argued that the retreat of an institution from certain public roles to more private ones is not necessarily an unstoppable process that will lead to the institution's demise. He points to the parallel example of the family. Family life also no longer plays as public a role as it once did, nor is as "extended" as it once was; but it shows no signs of disappearing. Rather, despite all the strains on the nuclear, personal-life family that remain, people continue to marry and remarry. They move out of the family as autonomous individuals into the work a day world, then at the end of the day withdraw back into it as the venue of personal, private life.

Family and personal life on the one hand, and public and occupational life on the other, are today separable and detached in a way unimaginable even a hundred years ago, when the family farm, the family business, the home above the shop, and family ties helping one get ahead whether prince or commoner were the way of the world. Now all these are pale shadows of their former power. Husband and wife are each more likely to be autonomous persons, and their children after them, in the business and professional world; whether one happens to live in family or not in one's off hours means relatively little professionally now.

Yet for all that, the family lives on in the personal sphere. Can this be a message, Smith implies, for the future of religion? Perhaps secularization, like "defamilization," can proceed only so far in the human world as we know it.[23]

The obvious difference, however, is that the family has a base in biological and nurturing imperatives that most people, despite proposed alternatives, seem to find compelling. We have noted certain of them in connection with the emergence of the species; religion itself seems only to afford them sanctions. The sociobiologists notwithstanding, religion apparently has no imperative of itself on quite the same level as that which sets men and women in families; it is either more personal or more social. Its real role, if our approach is correct, is in reifying images connecting subjectivity with our universal and infinite environment to make it humanly meaningful. Its ultimate future depends on the continuing need for such images, which can be a bit more subtle than Wilson's old-fashioned supernatural and far less trapped in sociological reductionism than Durkheimian social effervescence. Science and art have thus far not been able fully to duplicate them in the lab or the studio, despite strenuous efforts, less by scientists

St. Patrick's Cathedral. Photograph by Chris Sheridan.

and artists than by philosophers and popularizers of science and art.

Let us sum up the discussion so far. Virtually all secularizationists would agree that, as far as its visible moral and institutional impact is concerned, religion has progressively withdrawn from several major areas of human life in recent centuries, though much difference obtains on whether this is a general or special phenomenon and whether it is reversible. Richard K. Fenn has offered a detailed model for this process, indicating five major stages by which religion moves from being an undifferentiated cement of society as a whole to the increasingly "privatized" faith of many moderns.[24] We shall glance at it with a view to seeing how it may fit in with our model of religious history. The five stages are:

Separation of Distinct Religious Institutions

Although the separation of religion from the rest of society has undoubtedly been on course since the first steps toward division of labor, which may have included the setting apart of shamans as specialists in the sacred, this first step in the secularization process can be associated in particular with the appearance of the Great Religions. Despite their important imperial and other alliances, they consummately were religions that saw themselves as having no necessary connection with other institutions, especially in their international and cross-cultural aspects, for their scriptures, hierarchies, and institutions were essentially self-perpetuating, moving from one dynasty or society to another and enduring both persecution and patronage.

Demand for Clarification of the Boundaries between Religious and Secular Issues

The final word of this heading, *issues,* must not be overlooked, for the point is not now a general sense of religious distinctiveness, rather than a kind of language of a piece with any other, but a precise sorting out of what can be said with each tongue. What belongs to God and what to Caesar? What to the City of God and what to the City of the World? This was very much the task of both the medieval (devotional) and reformation stages in all religions. In the Middle Ages it involved residual church-and-state issues left over from the imperial alliance, such as the investiture controversy in Europe, and on a deeper level the definition of sacred and profane space within the psyche. Thus chivalry and devotionalism's long fascination with the parameters of human and divine love, and a broader distinction between inner and outer religion. The latter issue, long coming to a boil in the devotional cauldron, eventuated in the Reformation's characteristic emphasis on inward faith and "disenchantment" of the outer world. The result was increasingly sharp distinctions in practice, and often in theory, between the spheres of church and state, religion and science, or capitalist economics and charity.

Development of Generalized Beliefs and Values That Transcend the Potential Conflict between the Larger Society and Its Component Parts

The boundary clarification between the sacred and the secular leaves a wound, for society is no longer unified under a single, implemented world view. This calls for the discovery of new world views that are nonreligious, or only nominally religious, but that embrace both now-compartmentalized traditional religion and the separated aspects of state and society. By our schema, they are the products of a rationalist enlightenment that tends to follow, as a sort of reaction, the initial reformation ferment. In the Christian West it is represented by the democratic, and later socialist and Marxist, ideologies stemming ultimately from the values of that era, and also by civil religion; in the East, by the secularized and politicized Neo-Confucianism that became the official ideology of the Tokugawa regime in Japan and the Manchu dynasty in China, or the rationalized and universalized Hinduism of groups like the Brahmo Samaj and Ramakrishna Mission.

Minority and Idiosyncratic Definitions of the Situation

This step includes the attempt of "withdrawal" sects and cults to return to the undifferentiated situation for themselves at the cost of alienation from the "mainstream" settlement. Although sect formation has been a feature of religion at least since the Axial Age, and probably is always in part a compensation for the destructive side of secularization—also an eternal tendency, from a very broad perspective—it displays special proliferation in the stage just after ideology and civil religion have shown themselves unable to handle the situation with the degree of intensity and transcendent reference some demand. Thus nineteenth- and twentieth-century Christianity has spawned a vast array of revivalist and perfectionist sects, and within Catholicism "cults" such as those of the Sacred Heart and apparitions of Our Lady, each producing on a small scale a total, undifferentiated world of meaning based on one-pointed emotional focus and consistent life-style. Similar movements in the East, such as bhakti cults and the "new religions" of China and Japan, could be cited.

The Separation of the Individual from Corporate Life

This suggests that the ultimate privatization of spiritual life as ideology and sectarianism alike fail to compensate for the loss of undifferentiated faith. This stage, if carried by everyone to its logical conclusion, would mean the demise of all corporate religious institutions and public symbols. It clearly has not been arrived at yet by much of the world, and empirical evidence to support that this is the final stage of the process is at best inconclusive for the present. It may represent the situation in the People's Republic of China for the great majority, and the subjective state of a substantial minority on the rest of the planet, especially such "advanced" societies as Western Europe and Japan. But whether their low level of religious participation represents acute secularization as a historical process, or the "ordinary" religious indifference that has always characterized a fair proportion of the human race when pressure to conform is off, remains to be seen. On a less acute level, this stage may correspond to our folk religion stage, which does not entail the dismantling of religious institutions as such, but does disestablish and privatize religion to the extent that it makes it essentially local, ethnic, family, or "popular" in its center of gravity, and separate from the other major "corporate" institutions of society.

I will now examine the same process in terms of human experience in recent centuries in five areas: economics, politics, education, art and literature, and religious institutions. We shall, I think, see more clearly how, in the Christian West, we are moving toward Fenn's last stage and our folk religion stage.

Economics

The great power that the Christian Church, and similar Buddhist or Hindu religious institutions, held in the economic life of the Middle Ages through its role as landowner and political, even military, force, and through such moral influences as the ban on usery, has become peripheral. Capitalism, as it replaced the feudal order so congenial to ecclesiastical hierarchical parallels, has no direct comparable investment by religion, though religion often has a dependency relation to it since its institutions require donations from capitalist sources. One can, of course, further argue with Weber, Parsons, and others that capitalism was fired in no small part by the "inner asceticism" of the reformation outlook, and that its values still have a real though unspoken role in modern economic institutions.

But the very fact that these values have come to be largely unspoken in religious terms, and have no other relation to religion except religion's dependence on capitalism's profits, contrasts markedly with the feudal situation. It would suggest that in this sphere secularization in the sense of a separation of religion from coequal status with a major other institution of society is in process, abetted by the devotional and especially reformation subjectivization of religion to inward faith and corresponding "disenchantment" of the world. The whole movement is a clear example of Fenn's demand for demarcation between sacred and secular issues, the economic order being declared secular (save as, of course, godly people might be working in it), even as the church ostensibly remained a power in its own inward realm.

Politics

The intimate though often uneasy medieval alliance of church and state has clearly given way to separation for all practical purposes. Even in those nations that still retain a nominal state church, its influence on day-to-day policy making is minimal, and not even predictable when issues of great moral or institutional interest to it are at stake. As in the economic arena, a dwindling residual influence may remain in the "values" of the state, as articulated by civil religion and the pieties of politicians. In terms of Fenn's steps, countries such as Germany and France, which once had robust state religions, have now virtually reached the fourth stage; they have seen the boundaries of religion "clarified" at the cost of severe national polarization, have passed through enthusiasms for surrogate national ideologies, and now it may be argued that even the "mainstream" religions of these countries are acquiring sectarian characteristics in their homelands. The situation is not identical in the United States, the Communist bloc, or elsewhere. But whether the situation is one of uneasy alliance, antagonism, or indifference, one can say that hardly anywhere do religion and the state meet as natural partners or equal negotiators. They are, rather, disparate forces, like creatures of land and sea, who would clearly prefer to be left alone to go their own way, but must occasionally meet at water's edge to admire or snap at each other. This is secularization insofar as the two are no longer parallel institutions, but of different orders; they retain, however, the power to affect each other. Agents of governments still arrest and kill troublesome religious figures, and these figures still rally the humble against what they perceive as oppression and injustice.

Education

In a comparable way, education has moved from being, if not quite the ecclesiastical monopoly sometimes supposed, at least subject to weighty religious input on all sensitive matters, to generally secular control and content in Europe and America. The rise of classical and scientific studies in the Renaissance, the establishment of public schools, and the end of mandatory conformity to Anglicanism in English universities in the nineteenth century were landmarks of this trend. Although some European school systems retain token religious instruction, most state-sponsored education is essentially secular; religious education must be obtained voluntarily in religious institutions. For many people, both those who applaud and those who fear secularization, nothing symbolizes and actualizes more effectively than this the peripheral character of religion in the "real" world. For nowhere has the boundary between religion and other issues been more carefully and restrictively drawn; surrogate ideologies more persuasively preached; religion pushed more into sectarian stances; and indeed Fenn's last stage of the privatization of religion more nearly approached, than in education.

Art and Literature

Perhaps no process of secularization is more striking or, one might add, more puzzling and deeply ominous for religion than the decline of the sacred in art and letters. Puzzling because what it really means is that over recent centuries religion has held less and less interest for the most intelligent and creative members of society, and for this no easy explanation presents itself except in arguments that are really circular. Ominous because one wonders with what sort of vigor religion can survive without the support of such persons. The pattern is clear: several centuries ago the bulk of great music, sculpture, painting, and writing in Europe was permeated with religious themes, as it was earlier in Asia. Today, although plenty of third-rate and derivative religious art is produced, and such artists as the early twentieth-century symbolists have drawn from alternative esoteric strands of spirituality, art based on the dominant religious traditions that could be called original and distinguished is minuscule. The European decline of the sacred in art has been irregular; although the nineteenth century brought forth little that was not highly imitative in religious music, painting, and architecture, with its various "revivals" of Gothic, Byzantine, and comparable themes (though some of it required technical skill), in letters it still gave us fresh religious visions as rich as those of Blake, Dostoevsky, and Hopkins. But in the twentieth century the harvest has been skimpier yet. With the exception of a few self-conscious traditionalists such as T. S. Eliot, the most powerful spiritual passions in the arts have been from women and men who seem more precursors of an age of privatized faith than church oriented. One could mention such persons of uncovenanted grace as Scriabin, Camus, and Le Corbusier.

Religious Institutions

Finally, we come to the decline of religious institutions which have attempted to parallel the other major institutions of society we have cited above. We mean, of course, the great national denominations and universal churches that in the nineteenth and twentieth centuries in particular established public identities, bureaucracies, and local branches comparable to those of a state, a major corporation, or a school system. Much evidence lately suggests that this pattern is slowly breaking down. In the United States, the supreme "denominational society," and elsewhere, budgets for national church offices have declined, tension and even schism is on the increase between local churches and the national organizations, and denominational loyalty is clearly less important to large numbers of people than in the past. Cross-denominational alternative structures both local and national, including electronic media ministries, often compete successfully with denominational churches, suggesting a move into Fenn's penultimate step involving minority and idiosyncratic definitions of the spiritual situation. The growing frequency of church switching suggests that denominational identity is fading as an important value. William R. Swatos has suggested that religion is reverting to its natural base, localism, as it seeks to preserve its identity against adverse trends in the general culture, trends against which denominations, precisely because they parallel the structures of that same general culture, with its national and international political, corporational, and educational entities, are ill prepared to defend themselves.[25] But such a trend, if large-scale and irreversible, would be no mere blip on the charts. It would signal a turning of the tide of major religious-historical importance, for it really suggests nothing less than a reversal of the dominant trend of Great Religions during their first two thousand years of history—a trend toward finding national and even international bases of power to which the local is distinctly subordinate, toward defining their spiritual culture preeminently in relation to the major elite culture rather than the local, and toward making the local outposts sites for the dissemination of a great tradition rather than primarily places for the definition of local culture. Making localism central could only mean that a Great Tradition was becoming a folk religion.

To this litany could be added more subjective aspects of the decline of conventional religion: Bryan Wilson's decline of general belief in the supernatural, the decline of religion as an important influence on mainstream intellectual life. With regard to the second, here let us only allude to the prospect that although *religion* remains vital in many places, *theology* seems to be taken less seriously than it once was by intellectuals generally, and even by the churches. Only a generation ago theologians of the highest caliber—for example, Karl Barth, Paul Tillich, the Niebuhrs—were known to the thinking public, appeared on the cover of *Time* magazine, and were regarded as at least significant, even by those of the intellectual mainstream who may not have agreed with them. Now, though theologians of the merit of Hans Kung or David Tracy have been at work and recognized in our day, one is hard put to think of any who have had quite the public or intellectual impact of those departed giants. Though they may equal them in mental power, the times have changed and the public reception of theologians is not what it was. Similarly, churches both liberal and conservative appear willing to proclaim their doctrines without the benefit of much rigorous theological work; increasingly one senses a populist mood in religion that tacitly rejects the benefit of such labors to authentic faith.

In short, we have a situation in which religion as an institutional force is losing power to affect economic and educational life on a large scale, and political life as well in most of the Christian world save in a narrow range of issues. Religion as a cultural force is losing power to influence the course of music, literature, art, and intellectual life. Furthermore, what many would see as the real foundation of religion, belief in the supernatural and its intervention in human affairs, has faded until few people in modernized society actively believe in it except for the special cases required by their own orthodoxy, or unless validated by science as parapsychological phenomena. But any need for such validation gives the show away as far as the continuing authority of religion is concerned.

Qualifications must be made, of course, but they do not seem to vitiate the overall picture. In the 1980s much was made of the political effectiveness of the "religious Right" in the United States, but its day in the sun appears to have been brief. In the Third World the set of attitudes and activisms associated with "liberation theology" will probably enjoy a longer life, but it often must be distinguished from the political role of *institutional* religion; liberationism sometimes can be seen instead as another version of the localist, populist folk religion that may be the gravedigger and successor to traditional institutional religion. It is a form of folk religion very different, needless to say, from the faith healing and holy wells varieties; but its presence should not be completely startling when we consider the sporadic but longstanding association of popular religion with radical, even millenarian, movements expressing the protest of oppressed classes—from the early Quakers to the White Lotus rebellions of China—movements that frequently had definite political agendas. Religion is clearly more powerful in politics, economics, and education in the Islamic world than elsewhere. I would argue, as we have seen, that this is because Islam, as a younger faith than Christianity, is now at a stage of development similar to that of Christianity in the age of the Reformation.

But looked at in terms of centuries, the secularization pattern seems undeniable in Europe and America from the perspective of what has traditionally been the form and role of religion. Claims that religion can survive in a chastened and personalized but nonetheless subjectively authentic state may be true in some individual cases, but do little to reassure one concerning the prospects of a society that religion once legitimated and in which it once flourished institutionally. We cannot forget that, although both Durkheim and Weber accepted the fact of secularization and regarded it as progress insofar as it brought a truer understanding of the reality of things, both were fearful of its human consequences if the transition from religious to scientific knowledge was not skillfully made. Durkheim feared social chaos without the bond of faith, and Weber the excessive bureaucratization of life as the social order was "rationalized" and charisma pushed along with the sacred to the periphery.

And yet . . . and yet . . . doubts nag at the bold assertion that religion as we know it is on the way out. It has too often been declared on its deathbed before, and there are those American statistics that seem to fly in the face of secularization. Forty percent of the U.S. population still participates in a religious activity weekly. People are converted, transformed, and reborn; they pray and give and enjoy the fellowship of spiritual assemblies as though faith were still in its prime. They experience gifts of the Spirit and anticipate apocalypses while the "outside" world goes on in its secularizing way. In 1978, 89 out of 100 Americans prayed and 57 out of 100 said religion was "very important" to them. And in 1976, 1 out of 3 reported having had a religious or mystical experience.[26]

True, survey evidence does show some trends unfavorable to traditional religion. Robert Wuthnow cites evidence indicating that, at least in certain geographic areas, belief in a conventional theistic concept of God, and in life after death, has declined 20 percent between the 1940s or 1950s and the 1970s. In place of it, he sees an upsurge of ideas of a "mystical" sort, which he interprets as claiming that "the very definition of reality itself is subject to human control," a perception that would make such mysticism highly compatible with Fenn's last individualizing step in secularization. Wuthnow is appropriately cautious in the use of such data, pointing to the complexity of "trends" in a country such as the United States, but suggesting that diversity can only increase in the foreseeable future.[27]

We have, then, a world of mysticism and salvation that shows no obvious sign of rapidly passing away. But this religious world is increasingly a *separate* world. It is sealed off by more and more profound barriers of language, interests, attitudes, and institutional style from the other worlds we live in that are shaped by science, technology, secular education, and "rationalized" government, politics, and economics. The world of faith subsists without much creative interaction with "high" culture, though it has no small rapport with popular culture, at least in the United States.

But even though this separate religious sphere is experiencing the decay of those institutional structures that most parallel the rationalized, bureaucratic state or corporation, we would be mistaken to imply it is merely slipping into infinite fragmentation. The new religious world does have its structures and institutions. Although somewhat weakened, denominations survive and their politics can generate quite a bit of heat. Cross-denominational and local organizations thrive, along with structures of leadership that, whether in person or in the form of the TV shaman, contain large charismatic elements and give much place to voluntary labor for the Lord.

Precisely because of features such as these, the structures and institutions of religion are becoming, in Weberian language, *less rationalized and more charismatic*, with such elements of rationalization as remain devoted not to the routinization of charisma so much as to its perpetuation as charismatic experience on the periphery of an increasingly rationalized world. Thus, in American religion the most obviously successful organizations—and these are in fact notoriously rationalized and bureaucratic on the operative level—have recently been those dedicated to evangelistic crusades and television preachers of great charismatic appeal.

This spiritual world, transmitted increasingly through the continual renewal of charisma rather than through routinized structures of education and institutionalization, has decreasing interaction with the "outside" intellectual and cultural domain. Its values, no doubt rightly, are felt to be unsympathetic as thought and structure yield pride of place to faith and charisma. Religious institutions abide, but their value is felt more as visible assurances of the mythos validating present charisma and experience, as perpetuations of an Eliadean *illud tempus* when faith was bright and fresh, than as major channels of the transmission of faith today. The transmission role instead comes to be dominated by popular books, magazines, the electronic media, and the family and social milieu. Formal religious institutions of the denominational type have increasingly less and less control of the forms in which faith is transmitted in the face of such local or charismatic media.

We shall next see what this state means for the present and future of religion in the Christian world.

Chapter 6

Contemporary Religion as Folk Religion

What does all of this come to? To what extent does it confirm our hypothesis that the Christian world is now moving into the folk religion stage? To my mind, a highly appropriate model could begin with Robert Redfield's concept of Great and Little Tradition.[1] What we have, I think, is a religious Little Tradition continuing unabated, though decapitated of a corresponding living Great Tradition. Briefly, the Little Tradition refers to the way of life of ordinary people; the Great Tradition to the ideas, values, and practice of the elite.

Let us review the essential features of this picture. Restricting our discussion only to religion, the Great Tradition of a society would refer to the dominant religion as it is carried by its highly educated elites, usually priests and monks (and only the cream of these). In traditional societies these persons can wield appreciable political and economic power, and may well be closely associated with the kings and aristocrats who patronize them and make their courts centers of Great Tradition learning and culture. The Great Tradition's version of the religion is highly literate, engaged in exegetical scriptural study and works of philosophical theology; it is transmitted through education of good quality. It exploits as fully as possible the Great Religions' potential as religions of a remembered historical moment, with scripture, wisdom, and a rich cultural system capable of export throughout the world.

The Great Tradition's institutional structures, needless to say, are highly routinized, but can produce persons of marked though generally conventional wisdom as well as placemen. Being aware of history because of its closeness to the literary heritage and the centers of power, the Great Tradition takes a long perspective and values institutional stability. It tends in fact to emphasize the historical rather than the cosmic aspects of the religious world view, to prefer intellectual sophistication to unbridled feeling, to mistrust charismatic personalities, and to value interaction with the society's "mainstream" cultural and social life. It loves excellence in religious art and architecture, and those who patronize such excellence.

The Little Tradition is, in premodern societies, the same religion as it is understood and experienced by peasants, who, being nonliterate, know things only as they are in the present or as secreted in myth. It has small concern with formal philosophy or history; it is oriented to cosmic rather than historical time, concentrates on worship and experience more than theory, and is basically transmitted through family and community and charismatic figures such as shamans, "holy men," and wise women, as well as the local priestly representatives of the Great Tradition. In the villages, however, the priestly representatives usually find they do well tacitly to accept as "implicit faith" the Little Tradition's understanding of the sacred.

The Little Tradition religion centers around such seasonal festivals as Christmas, around family and community folkways, around things that are *done*—for example, pilgrimage and rite—and nonrational experiences such as miracle and mysticism. All this, rather than the books and culture of the Great Tradition, constitute religion. Little Tradition people are likely to feel, fundamentally, that they cannot really affect the course of society as a whole or the politics and policies of kings and courts—except by provoking a miracle, that is, through a peasants' revolt, a revival, a crusade, rather than by rational means.

As Redfield emphasizes, the Great and Little Traditions continually interact with each other. The Little Tradition receives its fundamental symbols from the Great, even though it may accommodate them to its ageless patterns, making them cosmic, atemporal, and subjective rather than historical and philosophically rational. Saints become transcendent semidivine powers rather than historical figures, the cross a sign of sacred space as much as a historical event. The folk of the Little Tradition may perceive their coreligionists among the elites of the Great Tradition with a strange ambiguity, at once uncritically adulating them for their learning and hierarchical splendor and hating them for their relative wealth and prestige, and their presumed hypocrisy and self-importance.

For their part, the Great Tradition elite will look upon the Little Tradition with an ambivalent combination of admiration and bemused contempt. Sometimes, like the Slavophiles of Russia in the nineteenth century, they may pass through phases in which they hold that, for all its seeming naivete, peasant faith is somehow really deeper and purer than their own. At other times, with Josephite passion, they may attempt, heavy-handedly, to reform it up to their own standards. Sometimes rulers find it to their interest, or perhaps material to their own salvation, to patronize and take into their confidence an outstanding charismatic figure of impeccable Little Tradition background—a Gyōgi in Nara Japan, a Rasputin or Billy Graham. The Great Tradition ecclesiastical elites, however, are more likely to remain aloof from such a one. On the other hand, there are persons who genuinely and effectively mediate betweeen the two traditions, making the best of each accessible to the other, such as John Wesley and his Japanese counterpart, Ninomiya Sontoku.

As Redfield points out, a Little Tradition can continue with a vigorous life of its own long after the Great Tradition by which it was nurtured has vanished, and perhaps been superseded by another. The villages of Mayan Indians in the Yucatan that he studied, though superficially touched by the Catholic Great Tradition, still preserved Little Tradition usages grounded in the long-extinct Great Tradition of the Mayan empire. "The shaman-priests of the villages," he reported, "carried on rituals and recited prayers that would have their full explanation only if we knew what were the ritual and the related body of thought at Chichen Itza or Coba."[2]

For though a Little Tradition no doubt benefits from interaction with a corresponding Great Tradition, and without it is bereft of important potential for sophistication and flexible, creative responses to new situations, it has a capacity to survive indefinitely on its own level, continually renewing its charismatic wells and even surviving persecution.

Like all Great Religions in civilized society, Christianity has long had both Great and Little Traditions. Its Great Tradition, as both secularization theory and our hypothesis of stages in the life of a Great Tradition have hoped to demonstrate, has about run its course for now. But its Little Tradition, far from quickly following suit and meekly accepting the arrival of successor, and now secular, Great Traditions as evidence of its disconfirmation, shows every sign of preserving its own Little Tradition level of Christianity, and perchance surviving as long as Mayan religion in the Yucatan.

The Little Tradition style of religion is what has variously been called Peasant Religion and Folk Religion, and within the context of modern society Popular Religion. Peter W. Williams has made quite creative use of the category in a study of popular religion in America. As he accurately points out, the classic peasant or folk Little Tradition is only a "first form of religion we might call authentically popular," in contrast to elite religion or the religion of undifferentiated societies.[3]

Indeed, the distinction of popular and elite, in contrast to peasant and elite, may be more than a contemporary differentiation alone. William Christian, in his excellent study *Local Religion in Sixteenth-Century Spain*,[4] has like Redfield found two levels of Catholicism: a Great Tradition represented by the intellectual and institutional Church, and another which is local, timeless, legitimated by miracle, giving much place to spiritual cause-and-effect in the form of expecting concrete blessings in response to devotional vows made and kept. This Little Tradition religion was corporate as well as individual, not seldom expressing itself in communal religious acts mounted for such purposes as warding off plague or drought. Christian makes the point, however, that this style of "folk" Catholicism was practiced in the cities as well as the countryside, and by members of the royal family alongside their patronage of the Great Tradition, as well as by the lowliest peasants.

The clergy often had a strange ambivalent role between the two levels. They were certainly aware of popular-level religion. Priests were not unknown who promoted its cults enthusiastically, or even trespassed the boundaries of orthodoxy altogether by performing magical conjurations to dispel locusts or storm clouds in response to popular need. Most, however, may have held attitudes little different from those Christian reports among priests today regarding the local shrines favored by the laity:

> Even now the fierce pride with which some brotherhoods or town authorities guard the books of miraculous images, even from the priest, leaves no doubt that whatever canon law may say, local religion is theirs. The priests are usually from different villages. They often speak of local devotions with a bemused tolerance, occasionally wondering out loud about "pagan superstition." But when asked about the shrines of their home villages, the same priests speak with tenderness, excitement, and pride. For them the religion learned at home, embedded in the home landscape, transcends the doctrinal attitudes learned in the seminary, which they may apply elsewhere.[5]

This popular religion was chiefly the religion of local chapels and shrines, typically based on apparitions and miracles, and their associated devotional vows, festivals, pilgrimages, relics, indulgences, and special acts of penance or honor. This religion, Christian states, was popular in the sense that it was predominantly lay, though clergy participated in it. But it chiefly met the needs of lay life, especially corporate, community life, rather than the needs of the universal Church or the gifts of eternal salvation which were its prerogative.

It is not the case, however, that popular religion downplays questions of theodicy or salvation, but rather intertwines them deeply with more mundane matters of protection and healing. In another book, *Apparitions in Late Medieval and Renaissance Spain,* William Christian shows that the God behind appearances of the Blessed Virgin or the saints in this setting—as in later apparitions down to La Salette or Fatima—tends to be remote and quick to send punishment.[6] Yet the offences are often largely spiritual, such as blasphemy or failure to attend mass, and the boons which nonetheless accompany these hierophanies combine healing for the living with injunctions that prayers and masses be offered for the dead. Petitions from out of the Great Tradition, such as the Lord's Prayer and Hail Mary, are urged by the heavenly visitors, though in a way which seems to make them principally charms or symbols of implicit faith. On a deep structural level, a situation not entirely different obtains in popular Protestantism as well. Here too, in such traditions as the Pentecostal, one finds an intricate—though ecstatic—mix of supernatural healing, prophecy, and admonition, of joy in the Spirit and concern for divine protection against sinister forces imperiling the faithful. However, in a religious situation far more pluralistic than late medieval Spain, a simple identity of the local community and the faith community can no longer be assumed, as much as many popular religionists might desire that goal.

Popular religion today represents remnants of past Little Traditions, together with popular responses both of rejection and of utilization of the fruits of modernization and secularization. Bearing that in mind, I would nonetheless like to speak of modern religion in the Christian world as folk religion to emphasize the instructive parallels between today's religion and that of classic Little Tradition societies.

The differences between the two are obvious. Strictly speaking, modern religion is only metaphorically folk religion in the peasant sense. Most modern popular religionists are not genuinely illiterate and have at their disposal not just the rude tools of a peasantry but all the fabulous devices of a high tech age for travel, communication, and computing. But the fact remains that the Great Tradition *meaning* of literacy escapes them, even as does any message contained in the medium of the written and published word. For modern popular Christianity as for folk religion, religious communication from scripture, testimony, or preacher is *essentially* miraculous, experiential, and charismatic. The words of the Bible are miracle-producing charms, not historical texts whose exegesis requires persons of elite education; the revivalist or TV preacher is a shaman evoking an Other World of miracle and meaning, not a lecturer whose words require reasoned reflection.

This style of religion may seem at first glance vulnerable to the vicissitudes of history and change. Actually it is extraordinarily impervious to them, as in the case of the Maya. Let us survey some basic patterns of Little Tradition religion and see how well suited they are to favor the survival of religion on this level for long periods. They are particularly well adapted, in fact, to assure the long-term survival of the religion in the absence of Great Tradition institutions.

Billy Graham. Religious News Service Photo.

Transmission through Nonliterary Means

In traditional folk religion, this means the faith is passed on through folklore, community example, or oral and exemplary transmission from parent to child and from specialist (shaman, wise woman, local priest) to disciple. In modern terms, it means transmission by media that are either nonwritten (preaching, radio, TV) or outside the literary mainstream, by traditions and group attitudes essentially rooted in the local community, and by specialists who though they may be seminary trained are basically oriented toward perpetuating locally grounded traditions rather than interaction with the intellectual mainstream. This means, in our day, transmission through the electronic media, through books that though widely read are considered to inhabit a religious ghetto and never appear in national book review columns or on best-seller lists, and through the immediacy of a locally experienced religion from which signs and wonders are not lacking. Its personalities are legitimated more by charisma than education in divinity. All these marks work for survival, for they leave faith untouched by the vicissitudes of bookish culture.

A Local, Personal, and Experiential Quality

This feature is contained in the previously mentioned extraliterary style of transmission. That kind of religious transmission does not communicate ideas so much as trigger experiences. The words and gestures of such transmissions are condensed symbols that, in the familiar local cultural context, evoke paradigmatic experiences and images—from childhood, from earlier spiritual stirrings, from the conventional lore of the religion. The phenomenological sociologist Alfred Schutz, following William James, has discussed the various "subuniverses of meaning" that parallel ordinary "working" reality: the worlds of dreams, fantasies, play, and religious reality. Moving from one to another involves a sort of "shock," he tells us, like falling asleep or waking up.[7]

In the case of the religious world, a trigger symbol, as well or better than rational exposition, can induce the subuniverse in which the religion is true personally and experientially. It can make one know the presence of Jesus walking beside one, or feel the Spirit moving in one's heart. This process is crucial for Little Tradition survival. That religious tradition carries on because of its ability uncritically to accept the reality of its subuniverses in the face of potential disconfirmation by "working" reality, a disconfirmation that, as we shall see, increasingly weighs upon the Great Tradition as it passes through its numbered days. The fundamental reasons the Little Tradition possesses that survival ability are, first, its *local* legitimation, where disconfirmation may not have much conscious strength; second, its regard for words as triggers rather than as rational discourse; third, its willingness to balance the claims of rationality with those of personal life needs; and fourth, its ability to counterattack in the form of "folk" criticism of the rationalism that is, for the Little Tradition, a value based on foreign (that is, nonlocal and nonexperiential) classes, needs, and traditions.[8]

Specialists Who Are, Like the Mayan, Basically Shaman Priests Who Perform Sacerdotal Functions in Offering Routinized Prayers and Rites, but Who Derive Their Call from Subjective Experience

In the modern world, many if not most popular religious figures fit this description. The story of the "call" and initiatory experience is usually an important part of their mythos, and it is continually renewed by an appeal based much more on charisma (properly endowed in such an experience) than overt routinization. This allows for perpetuation of leadership essentially outside the values of Great Tradition educational institutions, though these may be used formally. Leadership is produced, then, by the same kinds of locally legitimated triggers that confirm and perpetuate the faith itself.

Renewal of Charisma in Movements such as Cargo Cults, the Ghost Dance, Revivals, or the Charismatic Movement

The Little Tradition can engender movements that seem to respond to new conditions on its own terms. We cannot here engage in a full discussion of such movements as responses to modernity, a matter over which an immense amount of anthropological ink has been spilled. But we should note that though they may ultimately fail, such movements do "buy time" for conventional Little Tradition religion in hours of crisis, indeed when the corresponding Great Tradition may crumble before traumatic cultural shocks. They can preserve essentials of the Little Tradition, sometimes for as much as several generations, by appearing to meet the enemy with folk religion's own weapons: miracle, charisma, and tenacious belief. The combat itself reinvigorates the blood of the Little Tradition, usually bestows enough victories to give it fresh short-term validation, and suggests that if change is imperative it can change in its own way under the aegis of signs and visions and anointed leaders—which also means that it remains the same. The survival value of this capacity is obvious.

Permanent, Visible Objects such as Amulets, Holy Pictures, and Scriptural Books, Regarded as Signs and Triggers of Religious Reality

Stress on symbolic "hardware" is one way the Little Tradition eludes confrontation with the Great Tradition's texts and rational thought, and its vulnerable relationship with other major institutions. Instead it concentrates on that which, so long as the religion itself lasts, is holy through its own self-validation.

The Little Tradition survives, then, because it avoids what the Great Tradition regards as the assurances of religious survival, the great texts, the intellectual tradition, and institutional solidity. The Great Tradition's dependence on word, considered as vehicle for discourse rather than as talisman, is its most fundamental distinction. The scholarly brahmin feels most secure with the Vedas, and the learned bishop with the Bible, the Creeds, and the Church Fathers. Their textual orientation need not be construed in any narrow, conservative sense; it is the charter of the theological liberal as much as the traditionalist, only the words (or their connotation) being different. The spirit has been well put by David Tracy as he argues that the evolving life of a religion can be understood as ongoing dialogue with its great texts, not just authoritarian submission to them.[9]

Yet the Great Tradition's word orientation contains a fatal Achilles' heel. It directly makes the religion's hierophany historical, and so distanced in time. Though the faith may have a Grand Narrative telling how we got from then to now, what happened "then" is nonetheless only a mediated experience. In Paul Ricoeur's phrase, the "immediacy of belief" is "irremediably lost." We half sense that words, in the literary sense of words understood not as charms that directly evoke what they bespeak but as symbols to be interpreted and analyzed, decolor as well as convey their reference. In Buddhism the second and less adequate age of the Dharma, after immediacy had passed, was that of dependence on sutras. As Ricoeur again put it, with the coming of the text, "we can no longer live the great symbolisms of the sacred in accordance with the original belief in them." The "primitive naivete" is forever lost, and we can at best only "aim at a second naivete in and through criticism."[10]

Indeed it may begin to dawn upon savants of the Great Tradition, as it has upon the postmodernists, that words themselves fictionalize. What the historical words of a Grand Narrative create is not the past but a separate reality—one may say a subuniverse—fabricated out of a few shards from the past. It pulls and nags at humans not because it is true, but because it is precisely other than what we know by ordinary experience to be true. This is no doubt especially true of those pasts that validate religions. Their other reality may even offer what the critic George Steiner has called a cultural equivalent of Jacques Cousteau's dizziness of the depths, an intoxicating euphoria more alluring than life on the surface.[11]

But the fact that this allure is constructed of an Indra's net of words will sooner or late also come through to those who approach the tradition mainly in terms of words. The cleavage of words from reality, though a subtle observation, is one eventually made in literate cultures. It is implied in all study of texts as texts, even when most traditionalist. The coming of this observation is the Great Tradition's own foredoomed nemesis; though its dark advent may wait centuries or millennia, it is embedded in the Great Tradition's own operating premises from the beginning, like hidden canker eggs whose spawn will eventually devour their host. A Great Tradition of a Great Religion, born of the discovery of history and living by the instruments of knowing human life as historical existence—narratives and institutions—likewise dies in history, the cause of death being the engorgement of too much historical time and overexposure to historical awareness. In the end it can avoid a postmodernist critique no more than it could fail to see its history as a triumphalist Grand Narrative in its palmy days, or both it and its critics could fail to claim a "modern" position of privilege from which to survey the world and its events.

The fictionalizing quality of words does not mean, in the case of the texts of a great religious tradition, that the original hierophany did not happen, only that it could not have happened for its original experiencers exactly as it is portrayed in words. Something behind the words is unrecoverable, just as "all the words in Shakespeare" cannot fully convey the experience of anyone's average half hour. Yet, as these realizations arise from textual and intellectual labors, a Great Tradition wearies itself in struggles against them; it is as much from the resultant lassitude as actual disconfirmation that it loses its grip on education, art, and its own institutionalization. Finally, its proud custodianship of the sacred words becomes an incubus it can neither love nor shake off. This tortuous passage amounts to a new Discovery of History, like the other a compelling loss of "primitive naivete" for those who understand it, and now a double loss, not only of the original preliterate vision, but also of the believing naivete with which a Great Tradition views itself and its mission at high noon.

Even in late afternoon, of course, one may faithfully try to recover the sunrise. The reformation is an attempt of a part of the Great Tradition, as well as of popular religion, to get back behind the words again; it works, but only at the cost of laying out new words that in the end become fresh chains of Grand Narratives and doubts. Whether a second reformation is a possibility we shall consider later.

The Little Tradition, at least in its pure form, has none of these problems. It depends, in the Zen phrase, on "transmission outside the scriptures" even while making a talisman of scripture. Yet it is thereby spared the verbal Saturn who devours his children and will live longer, centuries longer, than those who live by words. Although it cannot truly annihilate time and live eternally in the first generation of the faith, much as it may wish to, the Little

Tradition is able to produce successions of experiences—miracles, conversions, the presence of charisma—which give the sweet flavor of primitive naivete. It matters not, in this respect, if the Little Tradition's conceptualization of that first generation deviates wildly from the historical facts. The point is that for the Little Tradition sacred power is present now as it was then, doing works as great or even greater than in that time. Before that power, then and now are one.

In conclusion, then, we affirm that secularization theory is correct in its perception of the drift of things—but only for the Great Tradition. Insofar as secularization theorists have for the most part been chiefly concerned with the Christian world, particularly Europe and North America, they have essentially caught Christianity in its process of transition to the folk religion stage, which is the same as to say they are witnessing, and describing, the death agonies of its Great Tradition. What they have not fully comprehended, however, is that the religion's Little Tradition can survive such an event, and indeed seem little affected by it. Like Buddhism or Chinese religion, it can linger as folk religion for several centuries, until finally confronted by situations beyond its intellectually and spiritually enfeebled power to control, like those that led to China's Communist revolution.

This crisis, like all stages in the life of a Great Religion, has come more profoundly from the working out of processes internal to the religion than from external causes. Yet obviously no religion is immune to external history. We shall now consider what factors in the environment of religion in the contemporary world are most likely to affect its future, and what in the world to come.

Chapter 7

Tensions in Contemporary Religion

First we must remind ourselves that religion is chronically in tension with its human environment. A predisenchantment world, when the human and divine were in harmony and God himself walked in the garden in the cool of the day, is on the same plane as Eden before the voice of the serpent was heard or the golden age before Pandora opened the box. Neither can be precisely located anywhere in the time streams of ordinary history or anthropology. In the hard worlds of which they relate, the mutterings of Paleolithic shamans grumbling of taboos forgotten, and lost ancestral years when wizards were strong, mingle with the eloquence of Amos, the herdsman of Tekoa, recalling the simple faith of the wilderness to a generation at ease in Zion, or with the warm oratory of any contemporary preacher nostalgic for the "old-time religion" of the frontier revivals.

For religion characteristically appears as a voice calling to the present from out of the past, a past always construed by faith as simpler than the present, and—at least on the part of those in the past who were true believers—in closer, easier touch with spiritual power than the present. The religious past tends to become a time of miracles and godly heroics scarcely imaginable today. From this vantage point, religion, buttressed by its own Grand Narratives, judges the present implicitly through piety and traditions reaching back to that past, and explicitly in the sermons of preachers who evoke it.

131

The faithlessness of the present evil generation is set against the virtue of saintly men in ages past, the bumbling confusion of values today against the clear logic and resounding creeds of less apostate times. It matters not if the homiletic of those other days themselves, whether by Church Fathers or medieval bishops or Protestant reformers, evinces the same rhetoric; it seems the very nature of religion to dwell, not only amphibiously between this world and the Transcendent, but also between sacred past and ambivalent present, the bearer of tidings older and simpler than the moral confusions of our tempestuous days.

So it is that much of the dissonance perceived between religion and society today reflects no more than the current version of the way things always are. Of itself it harbingers no great change. Religion is always discovering sin and unbelief in the world around it, and nursing deep within its heart fond memories of other days. In the same way, issues such as science versus religion, or religion and pluralism, seem never completely resolved and never go away. Though of course they take modern guise, the fundamental questions—what can be known even to the unbelieving philosopher by reason and what must be added by faith, how do we reconcile the oneness of truth with the manyness of faiths?—have, like the poor, long been with us and long have received diverse responses. Their equivalents have dogged the path of religion since archaic times, and probably will until the end.

To be sure, some tensions may be peculiar to religion as it enters the last, folk religion stage of a Great Religion, when the line between elite and popular culture is roughly the same as that between religious and postreligious culture. And some challenges to religion in the modern world may be unprecedented, threatening the long-term stasis one would expect between folk religion and an increasingly unreligious great culture. One thinks of rapid population growth, increasing affluence (on the part of some), and the boom in technology, above all in the area of communications, so crucial for religion.

However, we must not fall too hastily into assumptions that any of this spells unique crisis for religion, beyond the crises engendered by its own history. Chinese religion and Buddhism, during their folk religion stage from around 1500 to 2000, also encountered sharp population growth and traumatic technological and geopolitical change, yet did not decline or die before their time.

Indeed, rapid population growth may only offer new evangelistic opportunities. It is well known that the affluent are often more religious than the poor, and technology can work both sides of the religion/secularization street. For everyone led to doubts by its seductions, another may be converted by electronic-media preachers or make the pilgrimage to Lourdes or Mecca by jumbo jet.

But the new factors have a cumulative effect, producing a reality perception that is a reality of itself. That is that the modern world is a very different world from that wherein traditional religion arose and flourished. This perception and the equally important perception, primarily by the Great Tradition elites, that traditional religion is no longer prepared fully to come to terms with that difference, is basic in the transition to folk religion.

Population increase together with technology has meant urbanization, the dislocation of people from the traditional village church or temple. In the great cities one must find religion where one can, in church or new religious movement tailored especially to the lost and isolated, or else give up on faith altogether. Either way, it feels different from the world one came from and has now lost.

Again, rich and poor we have always had with us. But the modern style of affluence conjoined with the new technology has generated a world of entirely different images of what wealth and poverty mean—if not of the subjective realities themselves—from those of the days when the basic texts and images of our Great Religions were laid down. It is no longer a world of shepherds, kings, and swords, but of forest-devouring multinational agribusinesses, fragile democracy, and the threat of thermonuclear war. People's fantasy images come as much from the world of urban life, with cars and high-rise sophistication dominant, as from arcadian paradises, and from *Star Wars* as much as from King Arthur. Religionists may argue that the fundamental human dilemmas are the same now as then, and no doubt they are right. But if religion is a matter of manipulating images that link subjectivity and the outer cosmos, what those images are specifically is not a negligible matter. If a lot of our inner images do not match those by which the prevailing religion endeavors to construct those linkages, a deep-level problem is brewing.

We may not always recall how new this problem is for most of the world's people, and therefore how chancy its upshot still is. As recently as 1900, the great majority of the world's peoples were ruled by kings and emperors; and the bulk of those people, even in Europe and North America, were peasants or farmers, close to the land and the agricultural year, far closer in important repects—including attitudes toward the sacred—to the Neolithic world than to that of their urbanized or suburbanized grandchildren. In 1900 the Asian and African bulk of the world's population was still barely touched by the existential crisis of the Discovery of History two thousand years ago, save as it was filtered through folk religion versions of their Great Religion, or had reached them afresh in imperialist or missionary costume. Now it has been forced anew upon them, sometimes by appreciated rising living standards, more often at least by "rising expectations," not seldom by the horrors of war, revolution, and new forms of exploitation, always by wrenching and confusing change. But especially as far as religion is concerned, we are still in a transitional generation from that world to the next. Religion typically lags behind technological and demographic change. It takes a while for it fully to sink in that the new way of being in the world is not merely superficial, but—like the Discovery of History—indicates the uncovering of fundamental new realities and the implementation of new human potentials that cannot but affect the way we link ourselves symbolically to the universe and Ultimate Reality. Religion can abide the lag of a few generations because of its aforementioned appearance of *always* coming out of the past, being *always* somewhat out of joint with the present. How long it can maintain this disjuncture in the face of the radical image shifts the twentieth century has imposed on humanity remains to be seen. The signs in much of Asia and Europe are not good for religion's future; in the rest of the world its symbols, broadly speaking, still seem to hold, though the Great Traditions, apart from that of Islam, are crumbling. (This means, Islam aside, religion is in best shape in the United States and the Christianized Third World: Latin America and Africa south of the Sahara.)

The new realities—urbanization, technological revolutions, explosive overpopulation, and the rest—are already here. It is a matter of coming to realize on the deeper planes of consciousness how much they separate our lives from the basic images underlying the religious texts and symbols we have inherited. City life, the new technologies, unprecedented affluence for some and a compelling dream of it for many others—the basic problem of this cluster for religion is that it has produced a prevailing and pervasive outlook, which may be called materialistic utilitarianism, that has deeply dyed contemporary religion as well as all other arenas of human life, but presents profound challenges to the very assumptions upon which religion is based.

Materialistic utilitarianism is one of those presumptions so basic to a culture—in this case, ours, both in the "developed" and "underdeveloped" worlds—that it is hardly stated, much less openly challenged. It is the dominant world view of the academy, though one less expressed in departments of philosophy than in the vocational curriculum. It is the fundamental rationale of capitalist and socialist institutions alike, and of their governmental counterparts. It hardly less informs contemporary religionists, whether of the "positive thinking" and evangelical individualist stamps, or social activists.

The basic premise of materialistic utilitarianism is that the measurable and negotiable individual good is the maximum acquisition of material goods or their direct equivalents, and the supreme social goal their optimal distribution, whether that is calculated according to need or deserts. A good society, then, is one in which the desires of as many as possible for as much material benefit—defined to include not only income but also such advantages as health, education, and security against crime and war—as can be had is met. That personal fulfillment essentially follows material benefits is seldom seriously questioned in the "real world."

Some thoughtful people, of course, may muse on the striking fact that happiness—not to mention the deep inward joy of the truly blessed—does not necessarily apportion itself along rich and poor lines. But no one knows what to do about such an awkward observation, unless to suggest that the rich, or the state, put still more money into individualistic psychotherapy programs.

The pursuit of material gain above all else is nothing new under the sun. But two interrelated features of it seem special to the age of materialistic utilitarianism that has come on the heels of technology and affluence revolutions. First, few if any venues for personal fulfillment or measurement of worth other than those covered by materialism as we have defined it appear in public culture. Second, in this situation religion is unwilling, and probably unable, to criticize meaningfully the *premise* of materialistic utilitarianism; rather, it addresses only the effectiveness of individuals in such a world and the justice of distribution.

Even culture—the love of fine books, paintings, and music—once thought to transcend wealth and poverty insofar as it could be practiced by poets and artists starving in garrets or street singers as well as their well-heeled patrons, now requires a solid investment. One is left out in the cultural world without costly stereos, art albums, word processors, VCRs and their paraphernalia, whether one is creator or connoisseur. Ads, commercials, and examples on all sides hammer that home day after day.

Conversely, very few people believe in the consistent renunciation of material or technological goods. The way of life of traditional ascetics or "plain people" is seldom appreciated as possessing genuine positive virtue in itself, though its instrumental value may sometimes be recognized. Contemporary monks, themselves reduced in numbers, still lead austere lives by the world's standards, yet inhabit monasteries that own cars and computerized mailing lists. Or renunciation may be adopted out of "solidarity with the poor," but more as an instrumental than absolute virtue, for one hopes that eventually the poor will be poor no more.

More likely wealth will be justified by church people, as it always has been, as enabling the church better to glorify God and do good in the world. Technology only adds greater efficiency to these age-old objectives.

Money therefore makes happiness, in any sense most moderns can really understand happiness. It makes accessible not only sensory pleasure, but also careers, lives, loves, families, successes—all that has comprehensible meaning. It is important to realize that virtually all bands of the political, economic, and religious spectra are agreed on this. The real issue between capitalist and Marxist, or individual salvationist and social activist, is not over the inherent goodness of money and materials, but over their distribution.

Marxists say that economics creates ideology and spirituality, and lays the foundation of happiness. Whatever they say, the actions of capitalists show they could hardly agree more. Political liberals and conservatives do not dispute the premise, only the manner of the state's involvement in distributive justice. The church, insofar as it is concerned with justice for the poor, assumes that the poor need more money and what money obtains—food, shelter, clothes, and on up, one supposes, to TVs and personal computers. Neither religious liberals nor conservatives are now likely to deny the assumption, though they may differ on the proper role of the church—political activist or charity giver—in achieving the redistributivist end.

Any idea that poverty could be a state of blessedness in itself, a favorite of preachers as recently as a century ago, is now hopelessly discredited. It is quite rightly seen for what it too often was, a means of social control through the pie-in-the-sky-after-you-die technique. Even the most conservative pulpiteers nowadays exhort their poor to get ahead, but to do it by nonviolent capitalistic means.

Without money in the materialistic utilitarian age, one is nothing, in the most negative sense—undefined, without place, at best only a potential. What poverty might have meant to a Saint Francis or a Johnny Appleseed is seldom considered in any depth, and such renunciants of technology as the Amish are at best considered quaint; often they irritate us more deeply than they ought to rationally, and we are not quite sure why. We profess pity for them because they have denied themselves "all the advantages" in terms of ranges of choice available to the affluent and uninhibited. But precisely what sort of happiness is guaranteed by the existence of such choices, or whether any choice in the materialistic utilitarian range truly brings ultimate happiness, is little known because little pondered in today's climate of thought—though these were issues much considered by classic religious thinkers from the Buddha to Augustine.

Materialistic utilitarianism has a way of not only shouting down such questions with its "quality of life" arguments, but of making alternatives to its vision of reality almost impossible to raise. If what we know is what is communicated through such media as television, and what we think is what can be programmed and data-based, through what crack in our personal noosphere could any thought of what *we* would be without these technological enhancements break in? If we ask that question at all, we are likely to find it disturbing and garner only dark thoughts for an answer. For the images of technological devices, as well as the images conveyed through them and the image of what knowledge and power means in a world controlled by them, are parts of our own ego, our own constellation of images. Whether or not they are disconnected from the Ultimate, they are parts of us; if any of our images are threatened or die, we ourselves look death in the face.

It will be argued that this is just the way it has always been. Since the invention of writing, certainly since Gutenberg, knowledge—including the ability to ask ultimate philosophical questions—has always depended on technology. It has always, therefore, had an economic and material base, and has been the particular province of an elite with the means and motivation to get access to it; a knowledge elite knowing, writing, and publishing; an elite oriented to words and their reproduction. The Gutenberg world was no doubt as circumscribed in what it knew how to think or inquire after by what could be put in books and words as another is to what can be quantified, computed, word-processed, or sent out over airwaves and spacewaves; both were consciously or unconsciously bound to the economics of their media.

But though there has always been a knowledge elite, in the past it has been offset by other cultures, popular and spiritual, which have presented other viable values and alternative ways of being human. For the present purposes we may simplify a complex society sufficiently to suggest that in traditional China one could encounter not only the Confucian mandarin knowledge elite, but also Taoist mystics pursuing nonverbal rapport with nature and subjectivity, and a vibrant nonliterate peasant culture of village gods and seasonal festivals. Similar patterns could be found in traditional societies generally. There were three ways: the materialistic utilitarian way of the knowledge elite and the economics of its knowledge which is power; the aesthetic and contemplative way of cultivated others, from monks to poets; the peasant way of those without substantial cultivation or elite knowledge and power but who must maintain a culture, as must all humans. Each of these ways had its own integrity and means of perpetuation. Although there was much interaction, none had to depend disproportionately on another for its existence, for each had its own means of survival and communication and could give as much as it got; each had its own quantum of popular recognition.

Now, however, the other two ways are clearly marginalized by materialistic utilitarianism in a technological age. Ascetic contemplation is simply made irrelevant, in no way presenting an image of human life that has any entree at all to the language or technology by which materialistic utilitarianism governs the souls of men and women. Aesthetic contemplation, the world of the artist, writer, and poet, is as we have seen subordinated by its technological and communications requirements to the values of materialistic utilitarianism for all practical purposes.

Popular culture remains the heir to the peasant way, and indeed is a last redoubt of religion in much of the world. Yet it is subject to advanced technology, and so to the money values and materialistic utilitarian outlook necessary to them. Popular culture, like peasant culture, is still composed of song, dance, festival, and the exhortations of shamanistic preachers, together with the endless verbal and behavioral clues that demarcate a people. But now these are communicated less by folk memory and community example than by the electronic media and computerized technology of the knowledge elite.

To put it simply, people no longer know how to entertain themselves. They have forgotten how to generate their own song, dance, and festival without radio, television, and department store displays, and they would be hard put to perpetuate a flourishing popular culture independent of them. The knowledge technician, the mystic, and the peasant are no longer three recognized and self-sustaining poles of the human order, each embodying a viable image of the human. Rather, the last two are crushed by the first. Materialistic utilitarianism ratifies the dominant cultural symbols that technology creates by making them the only effective means of communication. If one wanted to say that prayer or telepathy were better communication media than the electronic, one still could say it only through the latter, making them the real value symbol. And as religion should know, symbols and their communication are what counts.

Thus for all the communications advantages, probably short-term, that materialistic utilitarianism and technology can lend religion, they also cause very profound tensions, the resolution or irresolution of which will determine religion's long-range future. Because technological society costs money and makes money on an unprecedented scale, a technological society is virtually bound

Ayatollah Khomeni. Photograph courtesy of the Permanent Mission of the Islamic Republic of Iran to the United Nations.

to fall into the materialistic utilitarian way of thinking. Religion goes along, less as leader than as follower in this high-stakes game. But though it can play the game, whether it can ever lay down a trump is another question. Its cards were engraved, like the tarot, in another day, and it may be distracted by the empty place it feels in its heart for its children of the mystic and peasant ways. Tensions remain.

Some of these tensions, such as religion versus scientific knowledge, whether of the Copernican, Darwinian, or Freudian revolutions, have been much discussed. But in the last analysis they do not seem to have greatly affected the average man or woman's relation to religion. That is not really based on theoretical ideas about the universe and the origin of species as much as on personal and community factors.

We have suggested that another presumed tension, that generated by religious pluralism, may actually benefit religion as much as undermine it; it strengthens commitment in a competitive environment.

In the same way, the emergence of democratic society, and the growth of other social institutions parallel to religion in the political, educational, and economic realms, while helping to reduce religion to folk religion, have not overwhelmed faith.

But other more subtle tensions will affect religion, perhaps very grievously, in an age of materialistic utilitarianism and the marginalization of the contemplative and peasant/popular paths to it. These include:

1. Tension over whether religion is really able to produce anything of value when value is measured in materialistic utilitarian terms. Despite much talk of the success value of private prayer and the feeding-the-hungry value of religion-inspired social action, and despite the ability of religion to handle subjective needs for many people, doubts are likely to persist as to whether religion as such produces, in the measurable terms increasingly the norm of verification in most other human domains, from economics to engineering.

One can hardly measure answered versus unanswered prayers scientifically, or the good works of the devout versus those of the less so. Religion could not think in such a way and be true to itself. Some studies certainly have shown that run-of-the-mill religious people may be moderately healthier and happier than the nonreligious. But materialistic utilitarian criteria would still have a hard time with the side of traditional religion that exalts ecstasy and martyrdom over healthy-mindedness, and experiences of transcendence over life adjustment. Yet the rules of the game are basically set by materialistic utilitarianism for most people.

Robert Bellah and his coauthors of *Habits of the Heart* talk about American utilitarian individualism and expressive individualism.[1] Utilitarian individualism essentially seeks fulfillment in materially gauged success terms, expressive individualism in terms of realization of inner potential, whether therapeutic, creative, or relational. Increasingly, however, it seems apparent that, in the context of contemporary American society, both are manifestations of materialistic utilitarianism. Expressive individualism, hardly less than utilitarian individualism, requires symbolization in pricy therapies, the proper electronic paraphernalia of creativity, or the material ambience of a good relationship—in a word, money—to be socially serious. These authors cite de Tocqueville's belief that religion could counter extreme American individualism by introducing some social concerns. However, much of contemporary religion reinforces the individualism latent in materialistic utilitarianism, which in any recognizable form presupposes that material symbols are measured by individual shares. The social concern of much modern American religion is not insignificant. But it tends to conceive of the welfare of others in individual material or service terms, just as does the academy and the marketplace. Its fellowships are usually based on shared values, and needs for mutual support, among lives so understood.

A few persons of our day have lived lives that seem truly other oriented, nonmaterialistic, and nonutilitarian, not only through personal asceticism, but in what is even more difficult in times like these: through demonstrating a genuine compassion that nonetheless cannot be measured, or politicized, in materialistic utilitarian terms. One thinks of Mother Teresa giving herself to the sick and dying of Calcutta, or Peace Pilgrim walking the highways of America virtually possessionless to bear her message of nonviolence. They are at once criticized, marginalized, and made into icons.

They are criticized, as Mother Teresa has been for not articulating the problem of Calcutta's abysmal poverty in terms of materialistic utilitarianism on its most idealistic level; she has not denounced the political corruption that certainly has had a large role in the city's ills, nor has she called for political-social reform to assure a more just distribution of goods in the "city of dreadful night." Mother Teresa, however, refuses to do other than serve Christ in the poorest of the poor in the most direct way, by personally feeding and nursing them, seeing that those beyond rescue in this world pass out of it knowing they are loved, showing the love of a warm human face and hand over one dying of the effects of desperate poverty to be a greater gift than any lecture or law. Henri J. M. Nouwen, a priest-writer sympathetic to social activism and liberation theology, and also to Mother Teresa, acknowledges that she "never answers the many psychological and socioeconomic questions brought to her on the level they are raised," but rather, "like Jesus himself, she challenges her listeners to move with her to that place from where things can be seen as God sees them."[2]

These people are also made into saintly icons. Often, as is the case with Mother Teresa, it is by the wrong people for the wrong reasons. They think that her refusal to politicize her ministry means she is on the side of the materialistic utilitarian status quo rather than because, like God, she is unwilling to apportion out the grace and love that flows through her in its or any other worldly terms, but lets it fall like the rain on the just and the unjust alike. In the same way, pacifists such as Peace Pilgrim are criticized as unrealistic and ineffectual by those who know little of the terrible power of the meek, and sentimentalized by the sort of people who like statues of Saint Francis covered with birds. Either way, materialistic utilitarianism has no place for those few who truly live by other values, without even the pretense of proclaiming its characteristic kinds of political and social idealism, much less its crasser acquisitiveness (which, of course, can also be explained as for the greater good of all, in Adam Smith terms). They are men and women neither of the Left nor of the Right, neither liberal nor conservative, capitalist nor socialist, in the usual partisan sense. But like the supreme saints of all religions they live simply. Like a modern Hindu example, Ramana Maharishi, they lead all to ask the ultimate question, "Who am I?" And like Mother Teresa (or Jesus, whose disciples ranged from collaborating tax collectors to zealots), they give themselves in love to all who come, regardless of party.

But though this quality of spiritual life may be self-validating for those who perceive it, for most the materialistic utilitarian ethos renders it nearly invisible, and the conundrum remains whether, in such a world, religion can be seen to offer tangible benefits.

2. *The individualism latent in materialistic utilitarianism for a time produces its own return of religion in individualistic forms.* Because of the personal expression this calls forth, it may well appear to be more fervent faith than the traditional, communal forms that went before. As it emerges into the modern world, for example, Latin America seems to be embracing evangelical Protestantism or liberation theology Catholicism, both more individualistic (and in that sense, though not necessarily in any negative sense, materialistic utilitarian) in values than the traditionalist peasant Catholicism of before. These forms require an individualistic faith commitment and way of life.

But individualism in any context is a recipe not only for creativity and success, but also for tension, sometimes destructive and unbearable tension, between self and social environment. Even as religion seems to succeed through heightened individualism, it may also pay a price for the painful isolation of the individual and be subject to the perils of disconfirmation when religion does not "work" on a highly individual basis, when personal goals are not met, prayers not answered, personal social visions not enacted.

3. *Some tensions will be created by technological developments themselves.* We have noted that advances in scientific knowledge on a more or less theoretical level, such as the Copernican revolution or Darwinian evolution, may produce vehement religious debate but do not in themselves disconfirm religion for most ordinary people. If it is disconfirmed for them, it is far more likely to be by social and economic factors, perhaps coupled with technological change, which put religion in a bad light. The bulk of the urban working class in Europe became disaffected with religion in the broad context of the Industrial Revolution, not directly because religion was unscientific, but because religious institutions generally seemed indifferent to their plight, irrelevant to the new world of machines and factory whistles. Whereas arguments from science were used by antireligionists of the day, and science lay behind the new technology of the factory, it was only technology

that profoundly affected people's lives directly, and only it that created the ultimate conditions of religious alienation.

What of the future? Are there technological developments in the offing likely to have such a marked effect on religion in ordinary lives? Yes.

The great technological fact of the late twentieth century, the computer revolution in management and automation, is not likely to exert any great impact on religion. To be sure, certain philosophers have seized on this creation of "artificial intelligence" to hint that all intelligence is no more than circuits and electric impulses, requiring no soul or God to explain it. But no more than Copernicus or Darwin, this assertion is not likely to deter those who wish to believe that, however it works, human intelligence was made by God. Probably more important in the long run will be the lower-level but persistent tension with religious ways of thinking induced by the computer's strictly formulaic model of thought, implying over and over that only verifiable "hard data" and quantified answers count. Theology, unlike physics and mathematics, will not gain much benefit from the one-eyed console. Nor would any world wholly engendered by computer logic and governed by computerized medicine, production, and life-styles have a place for anything as incorrigibly uncomputerized as religion. But human beings are resiliently multidimensional, just as they can be lovably illogical, and it does not seem likely that God will be replaced in the human heart by even the most advanced microchip in the foreseeable future.

Another possible development, however, is likely to affect individual human lives, and their family and religious dimensions, far more deeply. That is the possibility of achieving near immortality for humans through medical means by reversing the aging process. As astounding as it may seem to those who have not been close to research in the field, it appears that managing the biochemical processes that bring about aging and death is feasible, and that sometime in the twenty-first century "immortality pills" or the equivalent, making life spans of many hundreds or even thousands of years the norm, may be available at the corner drugstore. At the end of *that* life span brain transplants to new, perhaps humanoid, organisms might prolong life unimaginably longer.

The impact of this development on society and religion is awesome to consider. I shall devote attention to it simply because I believe that this quasi-immortality would have far more impact on the future of religion than any other conceivable technological advance.

The first impact is likely to be prodigious upheaval as a world grievously overpopulated and near ecological disaster must confront the absence of death. By 2030 or 2040, possible dates for the advent of immortality, world population—barring a rapid fall in birthrate or control through famine and worse—will have doubled its 1980s level to reach eight or nine billion. At the same time, this world groaning with so many human beings could be less livable than today's world. Desertification, warming and climatic change, all disastrous to agriculture, and progressive depletion of natural resources, will have taken their toll. One can only hope the technology will also be at hand for colonizing other worlds with our teeming spawn, or else miraculously multiplying the loaves and fishes upon which we subsist. Otherwise, one foresees with dread the wars and holocausts needed to bring the population down to a number safe for immortals fortunate enough to survive the day of sifting.

But moving past the transitional horrors, what characteristics would a postholocaust society of surviving near immortals have, apart from its parricidal and fratricidal guilt? First, in contrast to most human societies since the era of the Discovery of History, it would be a society of fairly stable life-styles and institutions, for these change most markedly over generations, not within a single lifetime. By the time one reaches an age of several hundred years, one is likely to be set in one's ways. But the institutions of this new world may not include two fundamental to today's world—the family and religion.

A fresh world of immortals following a deluge of blood would have very few children. After the holocaust, humanity would have a virtually biological horror of population increase; indeed, each person would sense in any new human life a direct threat to his or her own most cherished attribute, immortality. This is not to say the children who do come would not be loved and nurtured, but genetics ought to be adequate to assure they are in numbers only sufficient to replace the occasional loss of an immortal to accident, or to support off-earth colonization.

With little of the reproductive imperative, and with fabulously long life spans over which to vary relationships, the nuclear family as we know it would be severely weakened, and might virtually vanish. One envisions instead perhaps an acceptance as the norm of shifting "living together" relationships between men and women over the centuries, possibly within the context of extended families or informal communes in a post-postmodern revival of the primordial clan. But a decline of the family could only militate against religion as we know it, for as we have seen, providing sanctions for family life and responsibility has from the beginning been among religion's most fundamental pillars. Now that wing of faith will no longer be needed.

Incidentally, immortality could also diminish at long last the individualism of materialistic utilitarianism. One might suppose that a society of affluent immortals would be an individualist paradise. But that is not necessarily the case. With the goals of individualistic materialistic utilitarianism so near at hand, its fondest dreams so close to reality in the defeat of deprivation and death, its demonic drive may actually lose power and its opposites return from repression. The new immortals will be a timid folk, desiring cautious and well-ordered lives, skittish of risk and danger with so little to gain and so much to lose. Knowing they will have nothing but each other, neither children nor companions in death for unimaginable years, they will draw close to those with whom they wish to share the long voyage. All this will deflate individualism and enhance yearning for close community.

Another pillar of conventional religion, the affirmation of life after death, may be much diluted in importance as well. Although the "immortals" will not, of course, be literally deathless, and indeed may acquire a phobic dread of the occasional accident or infection that could terminate a career of centuries—not to mention the act of human violence—posthumous rewards and punishments may come to seem so remote as to lose much of their force. They may, like virtually everything from before the pill and the holocaust, seem to belong to a humanity so different from present experience of what it means to be human as almost to belong to another species. Indeed, immortality could quickly push humanity in that evolutionary direction.

A group of graduate students in future studies at the University of Houston constructed scenarios based on the putative introduction of an antiaging pill.[3] In general they projected a stable society of cautious, peaceful people, among whom the family has disappeared, and governmental and economic institutions nearly so, as their functions are mostly computerized and automated. Within fifty years or so, they said, a well-run global community would have emerged among acquiescent and content immortals whose interests are mainly in education and recreation, and among whom relationships may be intense but are short-lived and nonintrusive.

As far as spiritual matters are concerned, the graduate students predicted that immediately after the pill was introduced, traditional religions would mount a campaign against it amid acrimonious debate over the meaning of life and the hereafter. (However, some liberal Protestants would accommodate themselves to immortality.) Church attendance, they forecast, would increase for a short time, then decline. Most people who could would, of course, take the pill regardless of what certain preachers said, and in ten years organized religion would be discredited and on the way out. Self-improvement and environmental cults, however, would grow. As the society of immortals matured, its chief spirituality would be reverence for life and the universe in a broad, noninstitutional sense.

Interesting as this scenario is, I am not convinced that it is the way things would go. Though they may find it subjectively disturbing, I doubt if conservative religionists will outwardly oppose the pill. Despite their antipathy to certain biological tenets such as evolution, they have generally accepted the "miracles" of modern medicine as God-given with less demur than many liberals. I imagine conservatives would do the same in this case, merely postponing judgment until the end of a much longer life than three score and ten; they may think themselves part of the generation that will not die till he come again. Over the centuries of waiting, though, belief in traditional religion may atrophy somewhat.

On the other hand, I doubt if all religion of a conventional sort is likely to fade as soon as the graduate students thought. People with fixed spiritual patterns are not going to change them radically solely because life is prolonged. More important, perhaps dimensions of religiosity other than family and the afterlife will abide and be enhanced by long life and prosperity on this earth:

relational ethics, mystical experience of oneness with God and the universe, human needs for penitence and festival. The ultimate source of religion, if our view is correct, is the need to connect subjective and outward structures symbolically with the universe as a whole and the Ultimate Reality behind it. This need will not disappear, nor will the possibility of expressing it in rite and belief and institution.

In fact, in the abeyance of family a desire for the sort of intimate but nonfamilial community that religion can offer may well burgeon. My expectation, to be explored further in the next chapter, is that in this brave new world religion may remain surprisingly traditional in language and symbol, but will develop fresh forms of expression, will quietly shift some ethical emphases to meet new social realities, and will strongly encourage tightly knit communes or communities as basic religious-social entities. How long it lasts, though, will depend on whether it does these tasks on a folk religion level, or is able somehow to rejuvenate itself as a Great Tradition.

4. Finally, a fourth tension likely to be felt by religion will be engendered by the postmodern, end-of-history experience. If the immortality pill is developed and some holocaust devours those for whom there is no room on its ark, these momentous events could not help but engrave on human consciousness very dramatically, and traumatically, a sense of the end of history as it has been known, and the start of something else. In that apocalypse all previous political and religious Grand Narratives will be seen grinding to a halt far more vividly than today, even to postmodernist philosophers, though something of the reality may already be upon us. The crisis, though deep, will be acute for the inner self-consciousness of all Great Religions deriving from the Discovery of History era; it will end that era as forcefully as Alexander and Jesus and the others began it. What kind of temporal consciousness comes next will depend on how much humanity needs a historical Grand Narrative, and how much an end to history and its terrors means a reversion to cosmic time.

On the other hand, tensions—one might say cracks—can be spotted right now in materialistic utilitarianism, tensions that may leave an aperture for the light of religion regardless of how the holocaust-immortality scenario goes. Their validity, of course, depends on one's view of ultimate human nature and its needs; but unquestionably many people will feel their effect in years to come, as some are now. Here are some of those "cracks" or tensions.

The conundrum that if religion does not always produce the affluent rewards that are the real good in materialistic utilitarianism, neither does the latter, forces one back to other bases. Religion inevitably prospers from disappointment with materialism, and even amid the most modern affluence materialism will promise more than it can deliver, and will lose in the end (even in a world of "immortals") to its ancient enemies, which the Buddha enumerated as old age, sickness, and death.

A need for real community can become acute amid the individualism of a materialistic utilitarian society. Many will want something deeper than the parallel individualisms that seem to be the best materialistic utilitarianism can do, even in marriage.

For many people, desire for cosmic or ecstatic experience is a strong hunger, and it is rarely met save through religion in a broad sense. For only religion can really validate such experiences as ultimately significant.

Thus we see that religion can fellow-travel with materialistic utilitarianism for a long time, but will do so basically on a folk religion level. For religion will enhance but not significantly challenge the latter's fundamental but almost unspoken assumptions about the nature of human life, biased as those may be.

But the fit will never be perfect between religion and materialistic utilitarianism, and eventually tensions between the two may come out into the open to throw light on other possibilities latent in religion. Traumatic events in human life, such as demographic and ecological crisis and perhaps holocaust, and the medical reversal of aging, may hasten a transition out of the age of materialistic utilitarianism. We shall now examine some more specific possible futures for religion.

Chapter 8

Projecting the Religious Future

What shape will the religion of the future take? To talk about the future of religion at this point means talking about God after the end of history—after the end of religious history as we have known it, perhaps after the end of human history as it has played thus far. We do not mean there will be no more religion, or humanity, but that religious and human life will not be understood as historical existence or process as it has been. Since the Discovery of History, the Great Religions that that turning engendered have proceeded by their own dynamic through the natural stages of their career on the stage of the world; and that dynamic is about exhausted. Though their future chronicles may be marked by events, it will not be history in the high sense of living out a self-imposed Grand Narrative by the might of internal energy. It will, except in relatively youthful Islam, be the scattered reactive happenings of a life in retirement after a vigorous career—unless there is rebirth. For God, if he was ever there, will not himself necessarily have gone into retirement with those Great Religions that were, for a brief span, his major spokesmen on earth. Perhaps he will be content with the sort of worship presented by folk religion or postreligion humanity. Perhaps he will call one of the faiths back to youth and vitality. Perhaps he will be willing to let humankind come of age in its own way, finding for itself what symbols of bonding to the infinite it needs in an age of immortals after the dependencies and historical passions and nightmares of childhood and bloodguilt have passed.

Thus far, indications in all these directions are in the wind. For the answer to the future of religion varies with the part of the religious world of which one speaks.

The Chinese quarter of the world's population, as its religious heritage fades at the end of its folk religion stage, may be becoming the planet's first truly secular society. Even its Marxism seems to be giving way to a pragmatic, nonideological approach to human affairs. The success of China in coming decades and centuries in providing social cohesion and meeting its people's subjective needs without Marx or God, or Confucius, will offer material for very searching critiques of religion and secularism alike, and may harbinger the future of religion, or the lack of a religious future, in the rest of the world as well.

The remaining three-quarters of humankind does not seem ready collectively to give up religion entirely, though needless to say its practice is often weak among them too. Hinduism will undoubtedly remain alive for several centuries, albeit on an uncreative folk level, if India remains a reasonably free society. Buddhism outside China has dwindled but not disappeared. Islam, full of reformation zeal, promises to be a potent force for centuries to come but, unless it takes unexpected new forms, appears too culture-bound to expand much beyond the 20–25 percent of the world's people it now holds. Even though its reformation period ought to mark an era of great intellectual and missionary activity, for reasons we shall soon note the times are not propitious for major mass conversions by any religion; and because of the distinctiveness of Islamic culture as well as individual practice, it spreads only with difficulty when it does not convert tribes or societies collectively.

Our chief concern now, though, will be with the Christian quarter of the earth. This is not only because it is likely to be the religion of most concern to many readers of this book, but also because, in our view, the most important religious happenings of the next few centuries will occur within Christianity or lands of Christian background.

First, however, let us lay out the options. What follows are, for me, the three most likely possibilities for the religious future, particularly in the Christian world.

A Pervasive Secularism, with Humanism as the Reigning Great Tradition Philosophy, but with Christianity Surviving for Several Centuries as Folk Religion, Then Fading Away, or Reduced to a Small Remnant

This seems the most likely prospect. Looking at the large sweep of history, it seems the way things are going. Despite the folk persistence of Christianity and other religions, one detects few signs that a religious Great Tradition, on the scale of those in the great past ages of faith, is regrouping anywhere. That which is to come, from computerization to immortality, offers no different scenario, for as we have seen, although they will not be antagonistic to religion, their people should require no more than a folk level of it to give some content to a yearning for cosmic and communal experience. It may be noted that, even if Christianity is true, this outcome of the Christian presence in history could still obtain, for numbers and influence large or small neither prove nor disprove belief. Jesus asked, "When the Son of Man comes, will he find faith on the Earth?" (Luke 8:18), as though it were an open question. But we shall see.

As we have noted, secularism appears to be the direction in which Chinese civilization is going, and the decline of religion in the People's Republic is an extremely significant portent for the future. It is as important for the religious future as anything that could happen in the other quarter of the world that is traditionally Christian. Signs are mounting that the economic and political-military center of the world is continuing to move westward, as it once moved from the Near East to Europe, and from Europe to America. By the middle of the twenty-first century, when China's immense population and Japan's technological prowess have aligned, as they undoubtedly will, and reached full potential, world power will be centered in the west Pacific, and both the United States and the USSR will be powers of the second rank. When a culture area dominates world economy and politics, cultural and spiritual influence is not far behind. The example of the dominant world power as a successful postreligious society, if so it becomes, is bound to have a potent influence.

Nonetheless, it will be argued that China has never believed in a God or revelation quite like that of the Western monotheisms, and that, however lively its popular cults, its Confucian Great Tradition was always a secular philosophy by Judeo-Christian standards. Even if the Christian world is relegated to the second rank under the East Asian bloc, it is unlikely that it will spiritually capitulate. Although the West's Great Tradition may be, as it already is to a large extent, humanist in real values, popular Christianity will not disappear suddenly. (By humanism we do not necessarily mean the partisan antireligious version, but a general intellectual temper of disinterest in public religious discourse, and a tacit assumption that this-worldly human good and human culture is the public culture's center of value.) Folk Christianity will have its place for a long while, and when it fades, something else will take its place to offer symbolic links between subjectivity and the Ultimate. It may not even be something we would recognize as religion, conditioned as we are by the way the Great Religions have worked, but it will be a long time in inner preparation, it will seem to work, and it will be there.

A New Religion with a New Founder

Could the Axial Age be reenacted, with a new religious founder arising to create a new Great Religion for the new age on the scale of the old? The prospect is exciting and doubtless for some profoundly hopeful. And there is no lack of candidates for this awesome role. Over the last century or so many thousands of prospective founders have started as many new religions. Some of them, particularly in Asia and Africa, have drawn adherents in the millions. Yet thus far none of those claiming to be entirely new religions, rather than novel movements within older faiths, has shown real promise of becoming a dominant religion in one or more important culture area, much less playing the role of the Axial Age Great Religions. One doubts if such a religion could arise today or in the foreseeable future.

I think it unlikely that any new religion will ever again convert entire major societies to reach the status of the Axial Age Great Religions, or significantly alter today's religious map. Theirs was a religious era whose results we still live with, but whose time has come and gone. Denominational affiliations may shift, as they are

doing to some extent in Latin America, traditional tribal religionists may be caught up by missionary Great Religions as in
Africa, individual converts from one faith to another there may
be aplenty, but one does not envision a new Great Religion sweep-
ing across continents.

Why? In their expansion the historic Great Religions took in
whole populations because they were movements as much political
as spiritual. By converting kings, they gained the people; by becoming the ideologies of empires, they became one with a culture
whose weavings no one could escape. In our world of pluralism,
individualism, separation of church and state, and mass media,
where religious change is almost inevitably a matter of individual
choice and the options are manifold, it seems incredible that an
entire major advanced society would simultaneously move in one
direction. One sees no way modern society would radically recon-
stitute the religious pluralism it now enjoys. In this respect the
religious freedom contemporary societies take for granted must
be regarded as a conservative force, for it probably forestalls
massive religious change in the future.

Moreover, one fears that the sort of exposure afforded all
public figures today by the mass media would make the charisma
of a new founder, and the world viability of his or her movement,
harder to establish now than it was two thousand years ago. The
mystery, the glamor of a personality seen only by some, and
reported in writing only years after his or her departure, in an age
when myth as a vehicle for meaning readily intertwined with
literal truth—this is no longer accessible to us. Imagine a Jesus, a
Muhammad, or a Buddha in modern dress, featured regularly on
the evening news, and subject to the labors of investigative report-
ers. Perhaps they would remain intact as great and good persons,
as have a few contemporary heroes of the spirit. But whether they
would in our kind of world retain that numinous aureole that
makes them the subjects of theologies and the central symbols of
Great Religions that swept the earth is, to my mind, more doubtful. I am not sure our age could, or perhaps should, receive such a
founder as did the Axial Age. Its lines for the communication of
information are not right for the handling of new kerygmas and
saving persons; depending on how one looks at it, they are too
dense or too thin for such a burden. The best they can do is keep
the word flowing about those already established. The old Great

Religions may survive, even flourish, but it is unlikely new ones will be born.

A New Christian Reformation

This prospect would mean not only the survival, but the re-shaping and revitalization of one of the Great Religions in its folk religion stage. It would be unprecedented, perhaps unexpected and unlikely. But as I have stated before, the stages of a Great Religion are not to be seen deterministically, and I think this development is not impossible.

If a new reformation were to occur in a Great Religion to prolong its life, that religion would be Christianity. We will look at the reasons for this assertion in a moment. The new reformation would have to do what the first reformation did and even more, for at this point it would also have to do to some extent what the birth of a Great Religion does. It would need to revive the religion to meet new inner needs of a large number of people shaped by a new kind of society—one relatively labor-free and quasi-immortal—and release them to do what needs to be done in that society, just as the first reformation dealt with, and released, people experiencing a society shaped by nascent nationalism and capitalism. It may well be further required to find, like the Great Religions, a new symbol for spiritually understanding radically fresh ways of perceiving the human relation to time and the cosmos, a symbol as strikingly novel as once were the animal, the plant, and the transcendent person. This I believe Christianity could do. Of this more later.

First let us observe that, besides these three prospects—secularism and folk religion, a new founder, and a new Christian reformation—no other serious possibilities for the religious future exist. The human race does not yet seem ready for sheer secularism without the patina of a humanist ideology and surviving folk religion. It is nonetheless doubtful if religious affairs can go on just as they are without substantial change. In historical time everything of importance is subject to change sooner or later, even if a few islands "forgotten by time" may linger here and there; and in any case, religion is not likely to escape the demographic and ecological earthquakes already tentatively scheduled for the twenty-first century.

The dream of a few idealists of a world religion made up of some sort of combination of the present world religions is extremely unlikely. The actual dynamics of religious history strongly militate against this sort of syncretism. The religions, as we have seen, are at different stages of historical development and are not wholly compatible in cultural role. Moreover, historically we find that when current religion fails to meet current needs, the upshot is inevitably new revelation and new intensive religious movements, most often within an existing faith, not contrived syncretism on a large scale.

In the same way, the "universal mysticism" for which some have yearned—a faith centered on the teachings of the great mystics of all heritages, which they see as the true heartland of the spirit—is, for better or worse, not likely to become the tangible religion of the future for more than a few pure spirits. Mystical experience in itself is a profound and liberating thing, but it is individualistic. To have historical meaning, it must in some way be embodied in a social movement, which in turn will be governed by all the norms that rule the history of religion. If the mystical movement is syncretistic, it will suffer under the limitations just expressed. If it is essentially within a Great Religion, it will finally share its fate, though it may be the spark of a revitalization, even a new reformation. It may, on the other hand, be afflicted by the tacit—and ultimately futile—social conservatism implicit in many mystical quests. Those that do not align themselves to sects or waves with a strong social critique illumined by the beams of eternity, but are more eager to transcend than transform the world, in effect uphold the status quo.

Whatever happens then, after the current Great Religions have run their natural course, will be unprecedented and surprising, representing a new religious style as marked as that of any of the past's great spiritual departures. Yet, like them, it will maintain continuities with what went before. Indeed, like the Axial Age Great Religions, the new faith may make more of a show of continuity than is actually warranted by its intrinsically radical restatement of the human relation to the Ultimate. Its continuities may be like that of the Christmas tree to the *axis mundi* and annual renewal symbolism of the long-gone world of archaic cosmic religion. Its radical heart may be like the Christian revalorization of that tree to represent a historical pivot countering the discovery of historical time and its terror.

The most likely way such a new revalorization could take place, I propose, is through a new Christian reformation that, maintaining continuity with the Christian tradition, nevertheless dramatically reexperiences, restates, and resymbolizes human meaning in new ways.

In so doing, the new reformation will rescue Christianity from the doldrums of the folk religion stage and prolong the life of that religion a matter of centuries, probably beyond the demise of all other religions as world forces, and well into the age of the immortals. Beyond that our prophecy does not go.

But in the short term a new reformation within the Christian tradition appears the most likely solution—other than just letting folk religion and rising secularism run their course—to the crisis history will inevitably bring human religion. The new reformation is not the most likely prospect, but it is sufficiently possible to be interesting, and it deserves exploration. Let us consider why we would expect the reformation to be within Christianity, and not some other religion.

First, Christianity is the most genuinely world religion in world history, numerically larger and more cross-cultural than any other has ever been. It is thus the religious center of gravity, the tradition in which one would expect new developments of world importance to happen.

Second, Christianity has shown itself more continuously capable of self-correction and diversification than any other tradition, despite the fact that change has always been in tension with strong authoritarian and integralist drives in Christian doctrine, practice, and ecclesiastical life. This self-corrective capacity has been evidenced from the Protestant Reformation through the Second Vatican Council and is reflected in the immense variety of Christian churches spanning many denominations and cultures. It suggests a sinewy capacity to exhibit more innovation in the future.

Third, Christianity has shown itself adaptable to advanced, technologically complex cultures with open political systems. Apart from Japan, most such societies have thus far had a Christian background. This suggests that, insofar as successful future cultures are of this type—as they must be to cope with the problems already spawned by their present kin—Christianity is the religion most accustomed to dealing with them. Far more than the others, its leaders and thinkers have studied, written about, and issued statements on the problems of religion in the advanced democratic societies. It is clearly the religion most able to address the forces in the world making the future.

To be sure, one could argue, as many have, that Christianity, with its alleged doctrine of the human domination of nature, must bear no small blame for the evils of technological society and the ecological crises to which it is leading us. Its alignment with the technological world, they say, is not a mark of virtue but an alliance with Moloch that will lead to the discrediting of the faith when the bill comes due. Then perhaps the day will go to religions such as Taoism and Buddhism, which hold a better view of the human role on this fragile earth.

This is not the place to argue the complex issue of Christianity and ecology. We can only observe the social fact that Christianity stands with the societies that have made the world what it is, and will unquestionably make its future for both praise and guilt. Standing with them, it will be there as the available vehicle of the next spiritual step, if it is taken, even if it turns out to be another self-correction of prior errors.

The fourth point is admittedly still more subjective than the foregoing and is subject to dispute. Yet to me it seems provocative enough to be worth stating. That is a sense that Christianity, as it has developed over the centuries in the course of becoming the largest and most worldwide of the faiths, has become also the most universal in the sense of covering more fully than the others all areas of religious expression and experience. One can think of little that any of them possess, from contemplative monasticism to devotional fervor, from Zen freedom to Confucian moral earnestness to Islamic regularity of life, which has not also been answered in some version of Christianity—though to be sure those versions have not always been *en rapport* with one another. Yet they all do seem to come together in the teachings of Jesus himself, as they have been recorded in the Gospels. The religions of the world become, from this point of view, like a reference book explicating what was expressed by Jesus with mantralike pithiness. To understand what he meant by "The Father and I are one," we turn to Vedanta; for "The truth shall make you free," to Zen; for "Only one is good," to Islam.

If there was to be a new Christian reformation, it would have unrealized potential of this order to draw from.

A new reformation would emphatically not be merely a duplicate of the sixteenth-century event. It would certainly not be directed chiefly against the papacy and the Catholic tradition of Christianity, but instead could very well find essential leadership in future versions of these institutions.

Undoubtedly it would be strongly, perhaps centrally, grounded not in the older Christianities of Europe and Anglo North America as much as in the new, or revitalized, Christianities of Asia, Africa, and Latin America.

A new reformation would need to have a central theme, comparable to "justification by faith" for the first, a theme that both encapsulates the ideal of going back to the sources and offers an empowering experience in the midst of its own days. It could well focus on a discovery that was important to the radical reformation of the first upheaval, represented by such groups of direct or indirect Anabaptist background as the Mennonites, Brethren, Quakers, and Moravians. That is the centrality of the intentional Christian community.

Christian community is, of course, hardly a new concept. But the idea that, to be fully a Christian, one ought to live a shared communitarian life has rarely been fully explored since the early days of the church, recorded in the Book of Acts, save in monasticism and by the "radical" groups mentioned. This is because it seemed profoundly at odds with the Axial Age deep-level discovery of the individual as center of religious meaning. Faith thereby has given overwhelming practical preeminence to Christianity as an individual enterprise, based on individual belief and moral choice, expressing itself through individual labor in church and world, culminating in individual salvation here and hereafter. This individualism has major interaction with innumerable characteristics of our culture: capitalism, democracy, the materialistic utilitarianism of which we have spoken.

Yet individualism is not the only way of viewing human life latent in Christianity, as our reference to a few saints who have seemed untouched by materialistic utilitarianism may have suggested. The other way would be to emphasize first the vine and

Mother Teresa. Religious News Service Photo.

then the branches, the body and then the parts; in other words, to make the fundamental Christian discovery not that we are individuals, but that we find ourselves, that we live and die, in community—and this is the basic reality prior to any individualism. By community we mean a system in which the character of each individual is governed by its pattern of interaction with the rest, and by the interaction of the whole community with the environment. For humans many communities, of course, are givens, but they can also be intentionally constructed around determined principles. The Christian life, in this perspective, should be above all one that exemplifies the community reality perfectly through intentional as well as natural communalism, above all among those who share that commitment.

This new-old realization will fit the Axial Age criterion of a new discovery that is also one of which people say, "This was true all the time, but we didn't fully realize it until now." It is obvious and yet often ignored. But I would suggest that it may be the crucial realization of a coming new Christian reformation for several reasons, discussed below.

The first reason is scientific cosmology. Increasingly the universe is seen as an immense community rather than a collection of separate entities, however they may be bound by natural law. Newtonian physics favored the individualistic model by suggesting an impersonal, mechanistic universe in which the separate human could live an autonomous life gaining what he or she could from the universe by comprehending and manipulating its laws. Now relativity, general systems theory, and the anthropic principle tell us of a far more necessary and integral relation of the parts, including human consciousness and the universal whole, each depending on the other; it remains to implement such realizations in real human life through a communalist model of society.

Second, social change will favor decentralization of economic and social life. The revolutions in computerization, communications, and transportation will increasingly counteract urbanization to favor the decentralization of a growing population throughout the world's countrysides. This will encourage the sort of small, intimate communities in which religious intentionality can be the undergirding principle, making them also highly competitive economically in professional and high-tech as well as agrarian pursuits.

Third, on a subtler level, a realization that we are in a postmodern and posthistorical era will suggest the availability of new life-styles. Typical "modern" readings of history saw it as the projection of individual careers. The postmodernist critique of the Grand Narrative will lead to a diminished perception of history as the playground of "great men" and other individuals, and a growing realization that what is really important happens through the sort of interaction that makes and defines community.

Fourth, the Marxist critique is going to play a part in the coming world. For whatever its assessment in the so-called First World, the Second and Third Worlds, where it is powerful, will be part of what comes. Understanding in the Marxist manner that our views and character are shaped by relations of power and economic interaction with others, beginning with family and ascending up through social structure, will have a positive impact on seeing the importance of good communalism as a model of Christian, or any well-lived, life.

Fifth, communalism could be an end product of the diminished relation of church and state in a politically secularizing world. The freedom of religion from any obligation to represent the whole of society, whether as part of a de jure or de facto state church, will naturally enable it better to form alternative styles of life, including communalism.

Sixth, the most creative new movements in religion, from Christian liturgical reform to the Latin American "base communities," may be seen as possible prototypes of a coming new Christian reformation based on the community idea. On the operational level, community is becoming more and more clearly the most important form of Christian life and principle in many parts of the world.

Seventh, a new and dynamic communalism would be a practical response by Christianity to demographic and ecological catastrophes on the way. In their day propertied individualism will simply no longer be viable for most if not all people, and even traditional separate family life will be under intense pressure. On the other hand, experience of the various Christian communities in the

Mennonite tradition, such as the Hutterites, shows that communities can be workable even under highly adverse conditions. They can retrench; they can move from one country to another in the face of persecution; they survive.

Eighth, community life as a central value is profoundly at odds with the central values of individualistic materialist utilitarianism and therefore is well positioned to exploit for religion the "cracks" we spotted in it. Community will produce some real goods, in the form of personal satisfaction with life, that the other can never deliver in the same way just because it is a different way. It can obviously meet needs for real community rather than parallel individualism and can provide an appropriate matrix for validating cosmic and mystic experience.

To be sure, there are other possibilities for the grounding of a new Christian reformation. In our view a new discovery of the radical meanings of community would be the most likely theme of a new Christian reformation, as was justification by faith under grace and the enhanced subjective individualism it implied of the old. Some, however, might suggest that it would be liberation theology. To the best of my understanding, though, this identification of the gospel in part with social transformation through identification of Christ with the poor and oppressed is a means rather than an end, and the end would be precisely what we mean by community. Liberation theology, then, should be seen as a precursor rather than a rival of this reformation.

Others might speak of a new Christian humanism as an appropriate motif for a world of quasi-immortal and affluent beings, and a proper foil to a secular humanist Great Tradition. If this humanism were to stress both the centrality of this-worldly human good of the new humanism, and the emphasis on the artistic, intellectual, and traditional learning dimensions of the good life of the old Renaissance humanism, it would offer a valuable counterbalance to both the excessive otherworldliness of some Christianity and the one-sided politicization of life of some liberationism, whereby all art and culture may be judged in the Marxist manner for its alleged political content and revolutionary relevance. But again, it does not seem to need to be a matter of either/or.

The essence of community is realization that one is fulfilled not from within oneself as an individual, nor by material apportionment, but through what one gains by exchange with others and one's environment, up to the ultimate environment, Infinite Reality itself, or God. In Christian community, Jesus Christ is presented as the supreme symbol and guarantor of the validity of that realization, alike in his own relationships with others and with God. In Christian community, culture could never be the privilege only of those who have access to it by means of exploiting others and alienation from them; the liberationist critique of such culture is appropriate. But so is the humanist contention that much culture, of itself, addresses areas of human life other than the political. Thus liberationism again becomes a means rather than an end, a means to the creation of communities in which the whole of human culture is available to all and reveals its full meaning not as ways of individualistic enhancement but as ways of corporate realization through interaction. At that level it transcends politics as ordinarily understood; at that point liberationism, like religion itself, self-destructs before the heavenly Jerusalem. Humanism also is a means in the form of an ideal vision.

Needless to say, a new communalist reformation would not directly bring in such a condition, an ideal on the level of the Marxist withering away of the state, and like that one a dangerous vision if it justifies false means to a utopian end. It is important to realize that this reformation, like all such in the reformation stages of the Great Religions past, would be in practice partial, compromised, and subject to risk and change. We do not mean to imply that all Christians would join intentional communities. We may recall, first, that reformations are enacted typically only in one geographical area of the religion's sphere and affect the rest only indirectly and through reaction. Even in their area, they obtain a varied response, from intensive, radical enactment to nominal acknowledgment. This reformation would certainly be no different. It would be centered in a certain part of the Christian world, where some would implement it by forming intensive intentional Christian communities, others by trying to make "natural" communities more Christian, others by developing middle-level responses, intentional gatherings and processes within natural communities, on the level of the Latin American base communities. The important thing is that the idea of community and what it means would be the big thing talked about, struggled over, seen to be transforming lives and societies, and attracting the best minds of the day.

Let us, then, compare some of the new reformation's features with those of the other reformations in religious history.

It will grow out of devotionalism, in this case that of the folk religion stage, as the earlier grew out of medieval devotionalism. It will thus have an inner source far from the demands of a religious establishment or a Great Tradition, since these will be gone.

It may also begin with a newly acute asking of the personal question, "How can I be sure that I am saved?" though the answer will transcend the personal to embrace community.

Like all reformations, it will involve a putative return to the religion's sources, a rediscovery of the essentials, and the simplification of faith to a single, simple, sure key—in this case, the need to live in community. From that it may exfoliate into a new "scholasticism" detailing just what that entails.

The new reformation will develop in a way that makes successful participation in the emergent economic and technological life of its era not only possible, but easier than for those untouched by its grace. Just as the earlier reformation bestowed an "inner-worldly asceticism" that psychically prepared its lay adherents to be particularly effective capitalist merchants, and later industrialists, so ought the new with its communalism make its people especially well adapted to an age of quasi-immortality, decentralization, supercomputerization and automation, and perhaps space colonization. It will help defuse the problem of the nuclear family in the quasi-immortality age, provide congenial and effective economic units in a situation of computerized decentralization, and perhaps even provide ready-formed colonies for other worlds.

Finally, we must note again that reformations typically take hold only in one geographical sector of a religion, only indirectly or through reaction affecting the rest. If past history is any guide, that will be a region peripheral to the traditional centers of the religion's power, relatively lately converted, whose faith and culture was considered by some derivative, but with a strong and even militant sense of indigenous worth. Africa, perhaps also Latin America, come to mind as likely centers for a new Christian reformation in the twenty-first or twenty-second century. Europe and Anglo North America will probably be left behind, as were Spain and Italy in the old reform.

The new reformation will be more than a mere discussion, or enactment, of worthy sentiments about community. A reformation has to have its radical side and its doctrinaire enthusiasms. It wants to make a clean break with the past; call to its devotees, "Come out from among them"; and rebuild from the ground up. The new reformation will have its powerful voices who will cry that, to be truly lived, the Christian life *must* be lived in an intentional community with all things in common and all decisions based on the principles of the Sermon on the Mount. Such a community will be in, but not of, the world, facing it as a city on a hill.

These communities were foreshadowed by monasticism and such Mennonite-related groups as the Hutterites and Amish. The movement has been augmented by the twentieth-century growth in Christian charismatic communities and intentional communes of several stripes, from the highly communalistic new Bruderhofs to informal parish cooperatives for living and working.

If they are to be an important world-historical event, however, the new communalism must be much more than the old. Like the first reformation, it must open up genuinely new and challenging areas of thought and experience, lead to enriched intellectual freedom both communal and personal, and attract the best minds of the age. Whatever their spiritual worth, the older Christian communes (except the monastic) leave much to be desired in all these areas. Unless the new communalism boldly and stunningly enhances human thought and culture, and is seen even by its enemies as among the most novel and important developments of the age, it will be less than a real reformation, no more than another folk religion enthusiasm, and will dwindle away to nothing after all.

To make a reformation out of a bunch of precursors and enthusiasms it will take a crisis and a few charismatic leaders of the most major stature. Of crises the twenty-first century should bring plenty. Those related to extreme overpopulation, to the confusing sense of identity many feel in a pluralistic world and technological society in which one must go out and play many different roles, and to the ecological disasters that will be blamed on the way we have lived in the twentieth century—all will covertly point to communalism as a way out. So, if it happens, will the onslaught of hope the immortality pill will give those who survive.

The charismatic spark, the Luther or Chaitanya of this new reformation, is more difficult to predict. Will it be a public saint, the leader of a conspicuously successful Christian commune in a troubled world, the apostle of a pietistic movement flowing in a communalistic direction, or a persuasive theologian able to put into clear words simple truths widely rising into consciousness as things always true but unrealized? Will it be several persons at once? Or will there be no one, and the chance lost?

Either way, the course of religious history will flow on and on. If there is no new reformation, or if there is one after its age has run out, I expect that human religion will take forms, as we have already suggested, unrecognizable as religion in Great Religion style, with its highly explicit and well-articulated combination of doctrine, practice, and sociological expression, though the post-Great Religions religion may be somewhat closer to the undifferentiated cosmic religion that went before them. God after the end of history, in the Grand Narrative sense implemented by the discovery of history, may have something in common with God before history.

It might be better to say gods, however, for I suspect that what will happen when all the Great Religions have run their course will be an emerging experience of self and world in a way like that discussed by the archetypal psychology of persons such as James Hillman and Roberts Avens, previously mentioned. We will fixate less on a sovereign ego, a central heroic task in life, or monolithic symbols linking subjectivity and the Ultimate, than now, whether in individualistic materialist utilitarianism or in the programs of the Great Religions. With the end of sovereign ego, heroic task (whether success or personal salvation), and monolithic symbol, will go any need for the paraphernalia of religion in the Great Religion style, with its explicit and exclusive doctrines, rites, and institutions—not because of a utopian withering away of religion, as though the Kingdom of God had come, but because the linkage task is perceived from another direction. The other direction would be no new or radical thing: modern religious pluralism, the current tendency to see life as a series of experiences rather than as a single task, indeed all the needs we have spoken of as leading into a new communalism from the cosmological to the economic—all have led the way to recognizing a series of images (among which might be Christ and the Buddha) as coequally valid in a communal rather than totalitarian universe and heroic personal psyche.

This spiritual world, perhaps that of the quasi-immortals, would not reject all that religion has been or can be, but would tend, in the manner characteristic of East Asia, to see each concrete expression of it as nonabsolutistic and nonexclusive, so that one could move freely among its many images and practices, letting each correlate an image within oneself, a self-identity if one wishes, with the universe and Ultimate Reality. The spirit of Christian communalism, though this would not be recognized by those who will see it as a new reformation, would not be entirely inconsistent with that approach, for it will perceive the universe as relational and the personal psyche as a mirror of cosmic and personal relationships.

This spiritual universe would be a new thing, as new as the Neolithic compared to the Paleolithic, or the age of the Great Religions to either of those cosmic religion eras that went before. It could not be a return to the primal naivete of the former polytheisms or cosmic religion. It could not be viewed as a syncretism or universal mysticism based on the Great Religions, for it will be past their day. The coming from out of the One of this new galaxy of divine images, in which the old may nonetheless have an honored place, will be a fresh age of spirit.

Pointing to it, our word of prophecy based in the late twentieth century must cease.

Notes

Chapter 1: Religion Today and Tomorrow

1. Benjamin Franklin, letter to Eliza Stiles, president of Yale College, ca. March 1, 1790. Cited in Ralph L. Ketcham, *Benjamin Franklin* (New York: Washington Square Press, 1966), p. 177.

2. Emmanuel Le Roy Ladurie, *Montaillou: The Promised Land of Error* (New York: Braziller, 1978), p. 305.

3. Cited in John Gillingham, *Richard the Lionheart* (New York: Times Books, 1978), p. 36.

4. Le Roy Ladurie, *Montaillou,* p. 320.

5. Keith Thomas, *Religion and the Decline of Magic* (London: Weidenfeld and Nicolson, 1971), p. 173. See also Peter E. Glasner, "'Idealization' and the Social Myth of Secularization," in *A Sociological Yearbook of Religion in Britain 8,* ed. Michael Hill (London: SCM Press, 1975), pp. 7–14.

6. J. N. Findlay, *Hegel: A Re-Examination* (New York: Collier Books, 1952), p. 142.

7. A. B. Patel, "Sri Aurobindo and the Future of Humanity," in *The Future Vision of Sri Aurobindo,* ed. Sri Swatantra (Pilani, Rajasthan, India: Srijan Chetana Prakashan, 1972), p. 63.

8. Pierre Teilhard de Chardin, *The Phenomenon of Man* (New York: Harper Torchbooks, 1961), p. 273.

9. Ken Wilbur, *The Atman Project* (Wheaton, Ill: Quest Books, 1980).

10. Swami Prabhavananda and Christopher Isherwood, trans., *Shankara's Crest-Jewel of Discrimination (Viveka Chudamani)* (New York: New American Library, 1970), p. 110.

11. From the Gallup Opinion Index Report no. 130, *Religion in America 1976* (Princeton, N.J., 1976).

12. George H. Gallup, ed., *The Gallup International Public Opinion Polls: Great Britain, 1937–1975* (New York: Random House, 1976).

13. The following data are from David Barrett, *World Christian Encyclopedia* (New York: Oxford University Press, 1982).

14. Peter L. Berger, *The Sacred Canopy* (Garden City, N.Y.: Doubleday, 1969), esp. pp. 14–18.

15. Jacques Le Goff, "Mentalities: A History of Ambiguities," In Jacques Le Goff and Pierre Nova, *Constructing the Past* (Cambridge, England: Cambridge University Press, 1985), pp. 166–80.

Chapter 2: Religious Origins and Meanings

1. Henry David Thoreau, *Walden* (New York: New American Library, 1942), pp. 198–99.

2. Henry David Thoreau, *Journal* (New York: Dover, 1962), 8:134.

3. Jean-François Lyotard, *The Postmodern Condition: A Report on Knowledge,* trans. Geoff Bennington and Brian Massumi (Minneapolis: University of Minnesota Press, 1984), p. ix.

4. Ibid., p. xxiii.

5. Ibid., p. xxiv.

6. Jürgen Habermas, "Neoconservative Culture Criticism," in *Habermas and Modernity,* ed. Richard J. Bernstein (Cambridge, Mass.: MIT Press, 1985), p. 90.

7. William LaFleur, review of Herman Ooms, *Tokugawa Ideology,* in *Japanese Journal of Religious Studies* 13, no. 1 (March 1986): 107–15. I am grateful to this reviewer for helpful insights into the postmodern debate.

8. See Wilhelm Dilthey, *Pattern and Meaning in History: Thoughts on History and Society,* ed. H. P. Rickman (New York: Harper and Brothers, 1961), esp. pp. 129–30.

9. William Cantwell Smith, *The Meaning and End of Religion* (New York: New American Library, 1964).

10. Owen Barfield, *Poetic Diction,* 3rd ed. (Middleton, Conn.: Wesleyan University Press, 1973), p. 63.

11. Peter L. Berger, *The Sacred Canopy* (Garden City, N.Y.: Doubleday, 1969), p. 28.

12. Donald Johanson and Maitland Edey, *Lucy: The Beginnings of Humankind* (New York: Simon & Schuster, 1981).

13. Ibid., pp. 331–40.

14. Edward O. Wilson, *On Human Nature* (Cambridge, Mass.: Harvard University Press, 1978), esp. chap. 8, "Religion."

15. Johannes Maringer, *The Gods of Prehistoric Man* (New York: Knopf, 1960), pp. 17–22.

16. John E. Pfeiffer, *The Creative Explosion: An Inquiry into the Origins of Art and Religion* (New York: Harper & Row, 1982), pp. 210–25.

17. Mircea Eliade, *Shamanism: Archaic Techniques of Ecstasy*, trans. Willard R. Trask (New York: Pantheon, 1964).

18. Claude Lévi-Strauss, *Structural Anthropology* (Garden City, N.Y.: Doubleday, 1967), pp. 181–201.

Chapter 3: Religion and the Discovery of History

1. See Karl Jaspers, *The Origin and Goal of History*, trans. Michael Bullock (London: Routledge & Kegan Paul, 1953).

2. Karl Jaspers, *Philosophy*, trans. E. B. Ashton (Chicago: University of Chicago Press, 1970), 2:104.

3. The best introduction is Roberts Avens, *Imagination Is Reality: Western Nirvana in Jung, Hillman, Barfield and Cassirer* (Dallas: Spring Publications, 1980).

4. Owen Barfield, *The Rediscovery of Meaning and Other Essays* (Middleton, Conn.: Wesleyan University Press, 1977), p. 75. Cited in Avens, *Imagination Is Reality*, p. 26.

5. Barfield, *Rediscovery of Meaning*, pp. 60–61. Cited in Avens, *Imagination Is Reality*, p. 23.

6. The lessening of female power was not always the case in the first generation of a Great Religion, no doubt because at that stage it appealed to many, including women, outside the society's power structure and gave them place. Elisabeth Schüssler Fiorenza, *In Memory of Her* (New York: Crossroad, 1983), provocatively reconstructs the leadership role of women in first-generation Christianity. The Koran defined some previously ambiguous rights of women. Yet in these religions the spiritual significance of the feminine as such, whether in goddess or priestly roles, was countered on the symbolic level, and soon enough on the practical, by patriarchy.

7. Alexander F. Chamberlain, "'New Religions' among the North American Indians," *Journal of Religious Psychology* 6, no. 1 (January 1913): 1–49.

8. Ralph Linton, "Nativist Movements," *American Anthropologist* 45 (1943): 230–40.

9. Anthony F. C. Wallace, "Revitalization Movements," *American Anthropologist* 58 (1956): 264–81.

10. Neil J. Smelser, *Theory of Collective Behavior* (New York: Free Press, 1962), p. 313.

11. Bryan Wilson, *Magic and the Millennium* (New York: Harper & Row, 1973), esp. pp. 10–13, 485–89.

12. H. Byron Earhart, "The Interpretation of the 'New Religions' of Japan as New Religious Movements," in *Religious Ferment in Asia*, ed.

Robert J. Miller (Lawrence: University Press of Kansas, 1974), pp. 170–88. I have found both the basic idea and the bibliographical references of this article of great value in preparing this discussion.

13. See Peter Brown, *The Cult of the Saints: Its Rise and Function in Latin Christianity* (Chicago: University of Chicago Press, 1981).

14. James Hillman, "Psychology: Monotheistic or Polytheistic," in David L. Miller, *The New Polytheism: Rebirth of the Gods and Goddesses* (Dallas: Spring Publications, 1981), p. 120.

15. Brown, *Cult of the Saints.*

Chapter 5: The Modern World and Secularization

1. Emile Durkheim, *The Elementary Forms of the Religious Life,* trans. Joseph Ward Swain (New York: Collier Books, 1961). Original French ed., 1912.

2. Bryan Wilson, "The Return of the Sacred," *Journal for the Scientific Study of Religion* 18, no. 3 (September 1979): 268–80.

3. Peter L. Berger, *The Sacred Canopy* (Garden City, N.Y.: Doubleday, 1969), p. 107.

4. Joachim Wach, *The Sociology of Religion* (Chicago: University of Chicago Press, 1944), pp. 17–34.

5. Thomas Luckmann, *The Invisible Religion* (New York: Macmillan, 1967).

6. Berger, *Sacred Canopy,* pp. 175–77.

7. Peter L. Berger, *A Rumor of Angels* (Garden City, N.Y.: Doubleday, 1970).

8. Berger, *Sacred Canopy,* pp. 145ff.

9. Will Herberg, *Protestant, Catholic, Jew* (Garden City, N.Y.: Doubleday, 1955).

10. Robert N. Bellah, *The Broken Covenant* (New York: Seabury Press, 1975), p. 142.

11. Berger, *Sacred Canopy,* p. 145.

12. Talcott Parsons, "Christianity in Modern Industrial Society," in *Sociological Theories, Values, and Socio-Cultural Change,* ed. Edward A. Tiryakin (New York: Free Press, 1963).

13. Andrew Greeley, *Religion in the Year 2000* (New York: Sheed and Ward, 1969), pp. 97ff.

14. David Martin, *The Religious and the Secular* (New York: Schocken, 1969), p. 5. Cf. Max Weber, *The Sociology of Religion,* trans. Ephraim Fishoff (Boston: Beacon Press, 1963; original German source, 1922), pp. xxx–xxxi (from the introduction by Talcott Parsons), and chap. 1 especially.

15. David Martin, *A General Theory of Secularization* (New York: Harper & Row, 1978), p. 13.

16. Martin, *Religious and the Secular,* chap. 7, "Secularization and the Arts: The Case of Music," and chap. 9, "The Secularization Pattern in England."

17. Ibid., p. 22.

18. Martin, *A General Theory of Secularization.*

19. David Martin, *Dilemmas of Contemporary Religion* (New York: St. Martin's Press, 1978).

20. See, especially, Bryan Wilson, *Contemporary Transformations of Religion* (London: Oxford University Press, 1976).

21. Daniel Bell, "The Return of the Sacred?" *British Journal of Sociology* 28, no. 4 (December 1977): 419–49.

22. Bryan Wilson, "The Return of the Sacred," *Journal for the Scientific Study of Religion* 18, no. 3 (September 1979): 268–80.

23. Huston Smith, "Secularization and the Sacred: The Contemporary Scene," in *The Religious Situation 1968,* ed. Donald R. Cutler (Boston: Beacon Press, 1968).

24. Richard K. Fenn, *Toward a Theory of Secularization* (Storrs, Conn.: Society for the Scientific Study of Religion, Monograph Series no. 1, 1978), pp. 32–39.

25. William W. Swatos, Jr., "Beyond Denominationalism?" *Journal for the Scientific Study of Religion* 20, no. 3 (September 1981): 217–27.

26. *Religion in America, 1979–80* (Princeton, N.J.: Princeton Religion Research Center, 1980); *Religion in America: The Gallup Opinion Index, 1977–78* (Princeton, N.J.: Gallup Opinion Index, 1978).

27. Robert Wuthnow, *The Consciousness Reformation* (Berkeley, Calif.: University of California Press, 1976).

Chapter 6: Contemporary Religion as Folk Religion

1. Robert Redfield, *Peasant Society and Culture* (1956; reprint, Chicago: University of Chicago Press, 1973), pp. 41ff. The distinction is not new, of course; see Max Weber, *The Sociology of Religion,* trans. Ephraim Fishoff (Boston: Beacon Press, 1963), chap. 7, "Castes, Estates, Classes, and Religion."

2. Redfield, *Peasant Society and Culture,* p. 46.

3. Peter W. Williams, *Popular Religion in America* (Englewood Cliffs, N.J.: Prentice-Hall, 1980), p. 10.

4. William A. Christian, Jr., *Local Religion in Sixteenth-Century Spain* (Princeton: Princeton University Press, 1981).

5. Ibid., p. 20.

6. William A. Christian, Jr., *Apparitions in Late Medieval and Renaissance Spain* (Princeton: Princeton University Press, 1981). See also, for material on La Salette and other more recent French apparitions, Thomas A. Kselman, *Miracles and Prophecies in Nineteenth-Century France* (New Brunswick, N.J.: Rutgers University Press, 1983).

7. Alfred Schutz, *Collected Papers,* ed. and intro. Maurice Natanson (The Hague: Martinus Nijhoff, 1973), 1:207–59. See also William James, *The Principles of Psychology* (New York: H. Holt, 1890), vol. 2, chap. 21.

8. See the discussion of religious "triggers" and "condensed symbols" in Robert Ellwood, *Alternative Altars* (Chicago: University of Chicago Press, 1979), pp. 47–49.

9. David Tracy, *The Analogical Imagination: Christian Theology and the Culture of Pluralism* (New York: Crossroad, 1981).

10. Paul Ricoeur, "The Symbol Gives Rise to Thought," in *Literature and Religion,* ed. Giles B. Gunn (New York: Harper & Row, 1971), p. 214.

11. Interview of George Steiner by Bill Moyers in broadcast of "Bill Moyers's Journal" (June 1981). I am indebted to Professor George Tanabe, Jr., for this reference.

Chapter 7: Tensions in Contemporary Religion

1. Robert N. Bellah et al., *Habits of the Heart: Individualism and Commitment in American Life* (Berkeley: University of California Press, 1985).

2. Henri J. M. Nouwen, *Gracias! A Latin American Journal* (New York: Harper & Row, 1983), p. 58.

3. Jib Fowles, "The Impending Society of Immortals," *Futurist* 12, no. 3 (June 1978): 175–84.

Index

177

Index